Introduction

North and Mid Wales are blessed with some fantastic tracts of woodland. This is especially so in Mid Wales, away from the rugged grandeur of the mountains of the North. Here the many deep valleys and tumbling streams give trees the ideal habitat for growth. You will find both deciduous and coniferous varieties with one of the most amazing trees being the indigenous Sessile Oak. Whilst tending not to be very tall they counter this by having many contorted branches. Looking surreal in certain lighting conditions they seem to be from an alien land.

Coniferous forests exist in quantity but very few of the walks described here entail much walking through these. Not only do they tend to be very boring to walk through, mountain bikers use many of the tracks for their sport. *It is important to be aware of mountain bikers in these situations.* Felling of conifers occurs frequently, often meaning that tracks are closed.

The deciduous woods sport lovely wild flowers, especially in spring, whilst coniferous plantations and forests tend to have more sterile floors. In autumn the colours in deciduous woods are vibrant. Fungi and mushrooms are very common whilst in the more dense woods ferns and mosses, of many different types, flourish in the damp atmosphere. Misty sunlight filtering through the leaves and branches gives a mystical aura of a far off land. Woodlands give shade in hot weather when they become a good alternative to open hillsides, sheltering the walker from the sun's heat. It is not unusual to see squirrels, weasels or badgers along with many different species of birds as you walk. But take care – walking through woodland during or after a period of wet weather renders the ground, tree roots and stones slippery for a long time afterwards.

Some of the woods mask quarry and mine workings, hiding the scars of a bygone age. Although usually signed as dangerous it is *very important* not to enter any of these workings as they are unstable and often have decaying machinery littering the floor.

Whatever your level of fitness you will find, in these pages, walks to suit all abilities and tastes. It is not uncommon to have the routes entirely to yourself. All the walks follow rights of way and have been checked individually. However, changes do occur. If you find something that is incorrect please contact me via the publisher so that the walk in question can be amended in future editions of this book.

Each walk has a description and map which enables you to follow the walk without further help. The walks described do not venture high but some do reach open land before delving back in to the wood again. None are far from a road or village. Although a number of walks follow colour coded marker posts do not rely on them always being there. Adhere to the country code, wear boots with ankle support and, if you can, take a picnic as many walks have picnic tables. *Enjoy your walking!*

WALK I
FAIRY GLEN

DESCRIPTION A dramatic circular walk of a mile to an amazing river gorge. The river is extremely violent in flood when it should not be approached. Even in the dry the steps leading down to the river are slippery. This is a memorable place indeed. Allow 30 minutes for the walk but absorbing the scenery means a longer time will be spent here. A 'must see' place.
START At the Fairy Glen car park.
DIRECTIONS From Betws-y-Coed follow the A5 towards Llangollen. Turn right 200 yards beyond the Waterloo Bridge onto the A470, signed for Dolgellau. Immediately beyond the Fairy Glen Hotel, where there is a particularly fine Monkey Puzzle tree, turn left up the track leading to Cwmanog Farm B&B. This is before going over the road bridge, known as Beaver Bridge. The track is indicated as a Private Road. Drive through the white gate into the car park on the left 100 yards further, for which there is a small charge.

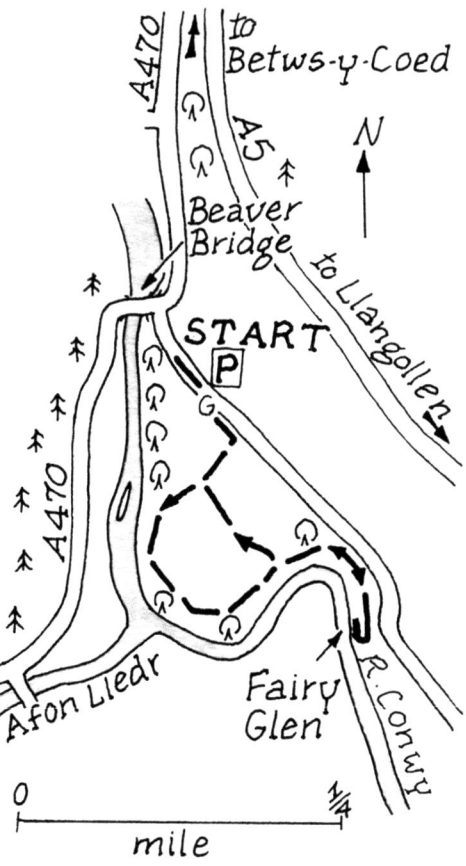

Turn left out of the car park and walk up the track past the access drive to Cwmanog Farm B&B. Almost opposite this is a covered gate. Turn right through this where another but smaller charge is made. Follow the gravel path to the left and then bear right past a squat chimney. The path descends slightly to a path junction. Go straight ahead, signed Riverside Walk. When the path reaches the river bank bear left and follow it to a 'Y' junction. Go up to the left and continue rising above the river to a seat by a multi armed finger post. Continue ahead following the direction indicated to Fairy Glen. More seats are passed to reach a steep, often very slippery descent down steps to a huge boulder at the river's edge downstream of the breathtaking Fairy Glen, a narrow deep gorge. To return retrace your steps to the multi armed finger post. Turn right where the exit is signed. Follow the fenced path to the next junction and turn right following the path back to the car park.

*B*eaver Bridge has below it a rather deep pool. Known as Beaver Pool it was at one time the home of a truly large beaver. It was frequently hunted by the locals. Arrows or spears were useless because of the beaver's thick skin and always evaded capture. An attractive maiden from the village was summoned to sing to it from the river's edge. Surely enough the beaver appeared and was so rapt it fell asleep at the edge of the pool. The hunters descended with ropes and nets to capture the beast. Aided by two oxen the monster was dragged to Llyn Glaslyn where it vanished below the sombre water never to be seen again. Perhaps, though, the pool was home to beavers at one time?

WALKS 1 & 2

WALK 2
COED BWLCHYHAEARN

DESCRIPTION A lovely 2 miles walk starting from the very pretty Llyn Sarnau. The path around the Three Dams Reservoir is very pretty indeed. There are some great views of Moel Siabod, Glyder Fach, Tryfan and a fine view looking over Llanrwst. Allow 1¼ hours.

START At the Llyn Sarnau (Lake of the old tracks) car park.

DIRECTIONS From Betws-y-Coed follow the B5106 to Gwydyr Castle. Turn left before the 'T' junction and drive up the road ignoring all turnings to the left and right to reach the Hafna Mine car park on the right. Continue past this to the Llyn Sarnau car park on the left.

1 From the car park cross the road at the yellow marker sign for the walk. Follow the track up to the right to a marker post. Turn left and follow the path to join a track. Turn left down this to reach a three-way junction. Go right and continue to another three-way junction where there is a marker post. Walk straight ahead by another marker post and pass Bryn y Fawnog, a house seen to the right. Continue up the track passing through a clearing. *There are great views from here of Tryfan and Glyder Fach.* As the track rises, so too are great views of Moel Siabod to the left.

2 Just after the track starts to descend turn right on a path marked by a post with arrow on the reverse side. Follow this path to the Three Dams Reservoir, a lovely place. The path continues around the left edge of the reservoir and crosses a partition dam separating the reservoir. *There is a fantastic view of Tryfan and Glyder Fach from here.* At the far side of the dam go left at a marker post. Follow more marker posts to join a track.

3 Turn left down this, then right at a marker post 150 yards ahead. Follow the path past an old mine on the right. The path descends through spoil heaps and continues down to join a track by marker posts. Turn right and follow the track until a small turning circle is reached. Turn left. Follow the path to the next marker post and then left to the signed Golygfan viewpoint – *with great views down to Hafna Mine and Llanrwst beyond.* Return to the marker post and sign. Bear left along the path to a marker post. The wide path turns to the left. Follow it down to the car park.

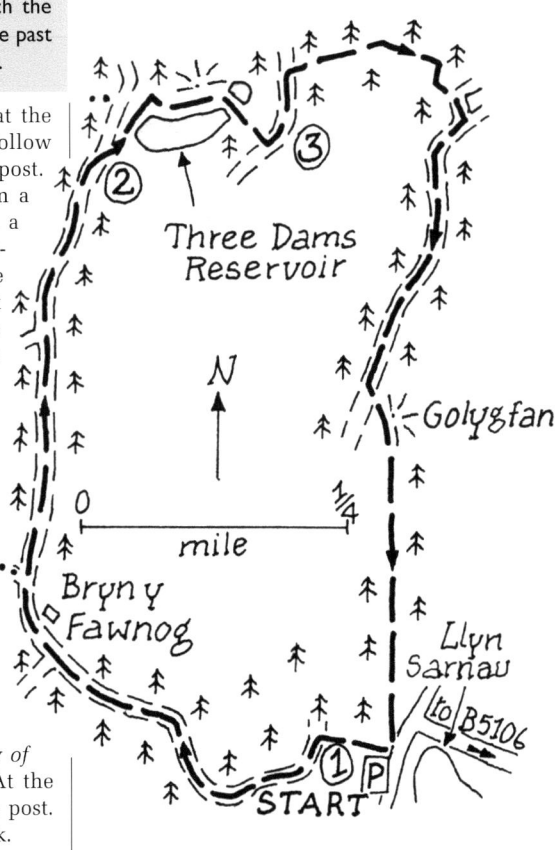

WALK 3
ARTIST'S WOOD & COED MAESNEWYDDION

DESCRIPTION This is a pleasant and easy 2¼ miles walk that takes in a small attractive waterfall as well as a lovely section alongside the Afon Llugwy upstream of the Miner's Bridge. Allow 1¾ hours. *Do not attempt this walk during or after heavy rainfall.*
START From the A5 at a large lay-by 300 yards before the Swallow Falls Hotel.
DIRECTIONS From Betws-y-Coed follow the A5 towards Capel Curig to where there is a large loop on the left, giving ample room for parking. There is a brown sign indicating the historical route and a parking sign here, 300 yards before reaching the Swallow Falls Hotel. Coming from Capel Curig the lay-by is 300 yards beyond the Swallow Falls Hotel on the right of the road.

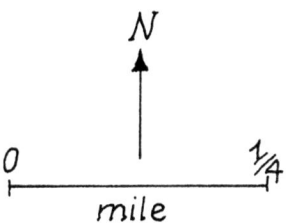

*A*rtist's Wood *was much favoured by artists such as Cox, Creswick, Pickering and Gastineau. The beeches here have regenerated naturally. This was also a haunt of the red squirrel, whilst the rare woodcock bred here.*

1 From the lay-by, cross the road and walk down the wide footpath alongside the A5 for 250 yards to where there is a wooden barrier on the left. Walk around the barrier and descend to a ruin. This was once part of the Pool Mine. Turn right. Follow the very scenic path, although often very slippery in wet weather, by the side of the Afon Llugwy to a footbridge. Cross this and continue more easily to where the path rises slightly and then descends gradually to river level. *The path alongside this short section of river is impassable during or after heavy rainfall.* Continue to a 'T' junction. Turn right, turning left leads to the Miner's Bridge, up to and around a gate to join the A5.

2 Cross straight over onto a narrow road. Turn right immediately and follow the narrow tarmac road steeply up to where the tarmac ends. There is a parking area here. Take the path starting from the far corner of the parking area and follow it up to reach a curved stone wall and viewing area. Cross the fine rustic bridge on the right to reach Garth Falls. Follow the narrow path up and away from the stream to reach a forest track. *There is a fine 'sharks fin' rock on the right.* Turn right down the track to reach a 'Y' junction.

3 Turn left along the track and follow it to a barrier across a track on the right. Walk around this barrier and keep on the track ignoring all junctions to reach a fenced forestry compound on the right. Continue past this and around a barrier ahead to reach a 'T' junction. Bear right and follow the track down ignoring the barrier on the left, to reach the A5. Cross over to the fine milepost on the wide pavement. Turn left and return to the layby.

WALK 3

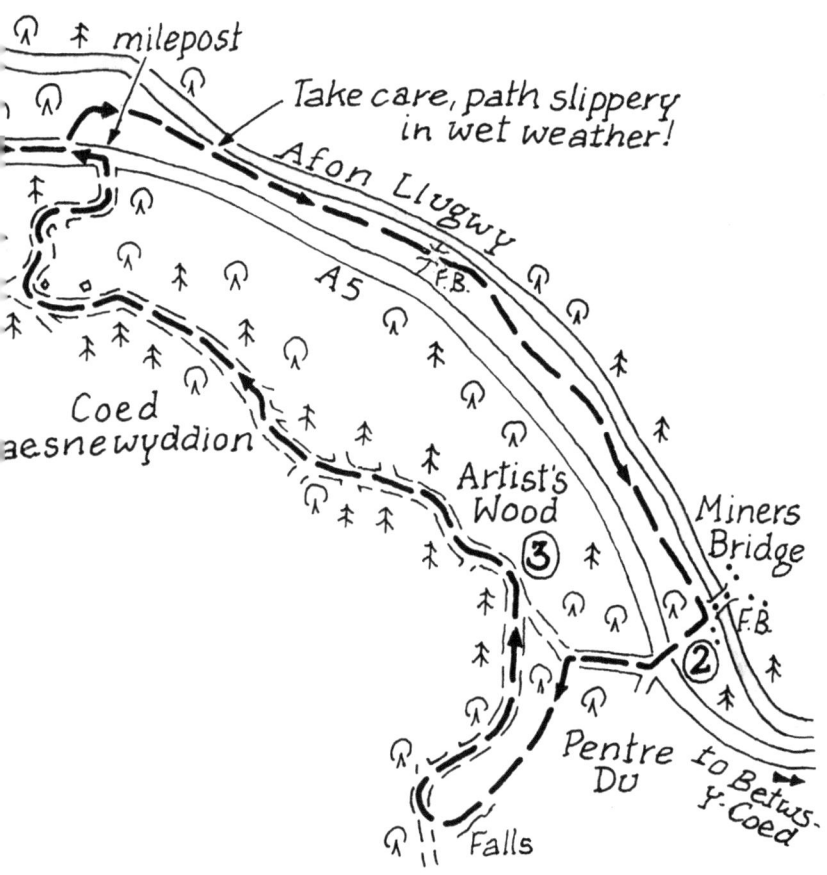

The **milepost** reached at the end of the walk is a fine example of a design by Thomas Telford where a metal insert was sunk into a stone pillar. A furlong is 220 yards. Travelling from London to Holyhead in 1815 would cost 6 guineas (£6.30) inside but half that for outside. Thomas Telford was the principal architect for the 260 mile-long A5. He also built the Waterloo Bridge in Betws y Coed.

By **the ruin** close to the Afon Llugwy are also the remains of a bridge. The bridge had a tramway across it serving the mill bringing lead ore from an adit 1400 yards long on the far side. Water power was used at the mill taken there by 12 inch pipes to a Pelton (turbine) wheel. The mine closed in March 1927 having been worked since the latter part of the 19thC whilst the bridge continued in use until 1952 when it fell into disrepair and closed. The mill was dismantled in the late 1970s.

WALK 4
GIANT'S HEAD & COED CRAIG GLANCONWY

DESCRIPTION A great 3½ miles walk starting from Betws-y-Coed. Although the start of the walk is along a quiet road it soon branches off to follow forest tracks. When these are left behind the walk finds a way along the high ground before descending close to a small and very pretty stream back to the start. Allow 1½ hours.
START At Betws-y-Coed Motors garage.
DIRECTIONS The garage is situated at the south end of the village on the minor road just after it leaves the A5 between Mairlys B&B and Cotswold outdoor gear shop. There is also a large sign indicating Betws-y-Coed Motors.

1 From the garage walk along the minor road until close to the railway bridge. Turn right at a marker post and barrier. Follow the forest track steadily uphill and around a zig-zag bend. The gradient eases briefly then continues steadily uphill once more and passes a good viewpoint of the Upper Conwy valley to the left. Keep following the main track up to a marker post and fence on the left below which is Clogwyn y Gigfran (Giants Head Cliff). Continue up the track past a marker post on the left until a hairpin bend to the left is reached.

2 Turn right off the track by a marker post on the right. Follow the path, which is boggy at first, to reach a gate. Go through this to enter the grounds ahead. Go right onto a track then turn immediately left through a metal gate. There is a blue topped pole here. Bear right and pass a marker post on the left and follow the path above Mynydd Bychan farm to where it splits at a 'Y' junction. Take the left arm of the 'Y' and walk uphill past a marker post on the left and go through a gate. The path continues up to another marker post. Turn right and up what was once a track to reach another. Turn right. Continue down ignoring the footpath sign on the left. Keep following the track to a 'Y' junction. Take the right arm of the 'Y' and follow the track down to a junction with another track.

3 Turn right. (However, if you wish to extend the walk, turn left here and follow the white markers to reach Llyn Elsi and walk around the lake – see walk 1 in Kittiwake Lakes guide volume 1. Follow the track down until a stream is seen to the right. Turn right 100 yards beyond at a marker past on the right. Walk down the obvious path and cross a footbridge spanning a very pretty tumbling stream. Continue down by the side of this crossing it again on another footbridge to finally reach the road at Betws-y-Coed Motors.

A rather gruesome story is attached to Mynydd Bychan dating from around 1750. It concerns a certain miserly old bachelor called Rhys ap Hughes often referred to as Rhys y Ceiliogod, Rhys of the Cocks. He was not in favour with the locals because of his penchant for the cruel, barbaric sport of cock fighting. One night he was in Betws-y-Coed drinking along with his housekeeper. On returning through the wood, much the worse for wear, they discovered on nearing their home that it was ablaze. It was beyond saving. Their grief was complete and expressed by much wailing. As such the site became known as Rhiwgri, the hill of weeping!

WALK 4

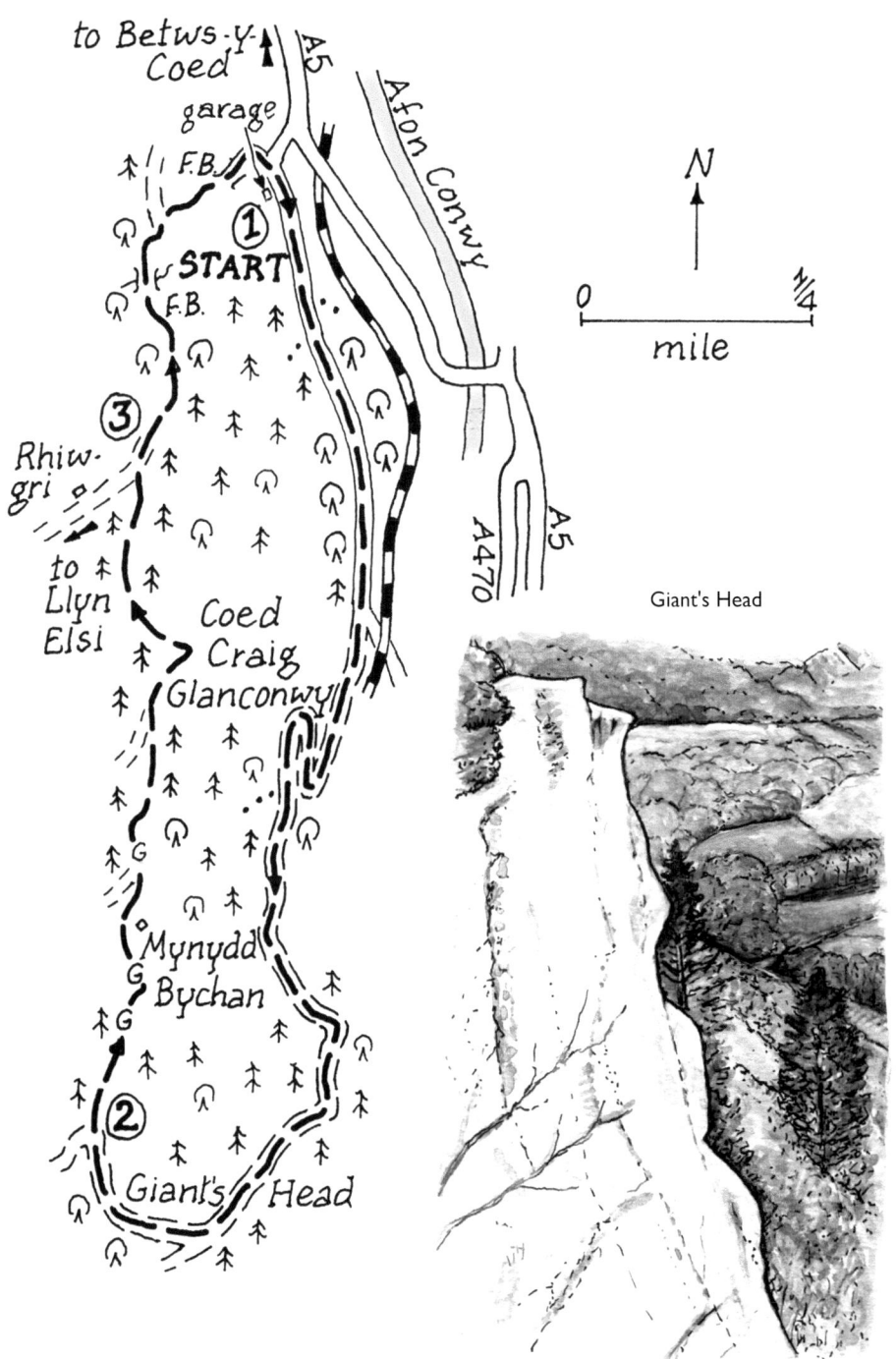

Giant's Head

WALK 5

COED ABERLLYN, PEN YR ALLT & COED DIOSGYDD

DESCRIPTION This fine 4½ miles walk is quite steep to start and enters some fine woodland with some impressive views down into the Aberllyn Ravine. A clearing at Coedmawr gives fine mountain views. After a steep descent a pretty cataract is passed. The walk alongside the Afon Llugwy at the end of the walk is delightful. Allow 2½ hours.

START At the Pont y Pair car park in Betws-y-Coed.

DIRECTIONS From the A5 in Betws-y-Coed turn onto the B5106 that leads to Trefriw. Turn left immediately after crossing the bridge and then right almost immediately into the car park. There is a small charge but there are toilets here.

1 From the car park turn right up the steep road. Turn right at the first road junction. Continue along this road to where there is a path indicator board. Turn left here following the blue titled 'Pen yr Allt' walk along the narrow tarmac road. Where the houses end the track splits. Take the higher one and follow it up to a marker post. Turn right up the rough path to reach a path junction. (The right hand one goes to Cyrau). Continue straight ahead up the path passing a blue ringed marker post. The steep path reaches a seat and continues in similar steep vein. Firstly right then left up the hill to a marker post where the path splits. Ignore the right hand one and continue straight ahead. At the next marker post by a small clump of boulders turn right and follow the rough steep path past a marker post to enter a clearing at another marker post. Cross the clearing to a marker post and descend to a fence passing it on the right. Follow the level path to a marker post and turn left along the track. Follow this to where the track rises. When the track bends to the left turn right.

2 Continue up through fine mixed woodland to join a forest road. Turn right at a marker post. Follow the forest road up and go across a turning area to where a path goes off to the left by a white marker post. Continue straight ahead on the track with a blue marker post on the right, passing a 'No bikes' sign. The track shrinks to a path where the Aberllyn Ravine is below and a waterfall heard. Follow the path to where it descends steeply but aided by a hand rail and continue past a ruin. Continue up to a level area and the next marker post at a junction with a track. Turn left up this. Ignore the path on the right after 100 yards. At a main junction after a barrier turn righ, with a marker post on the left. Follow this track for 350 yards keeping a careful eye for a marker post on the left. Turn left here off the track and follow the path up then down to reach a 'Y' junction. Follow the left arm of the 'Y' at a marker post. Continue to and over a stile. Follow marker posts through a short boggy section, some ruins and along a grassy path to the finely sited Coedmawr – *from which there are fine views of Moel Siabod.*

3 Turn right over a ladder stile by a marker post. *There is a fine view of Tryfan, Glyder Fach and Pen yr Ole Wen from here.* Follow the track for 120 yards and turn right at a marker post. Climb over the stile at a marker post and follow the path with a fence on the right – *with a superb view of Moel Siabod.* Continue to two stiles. Climb over

WALK 5

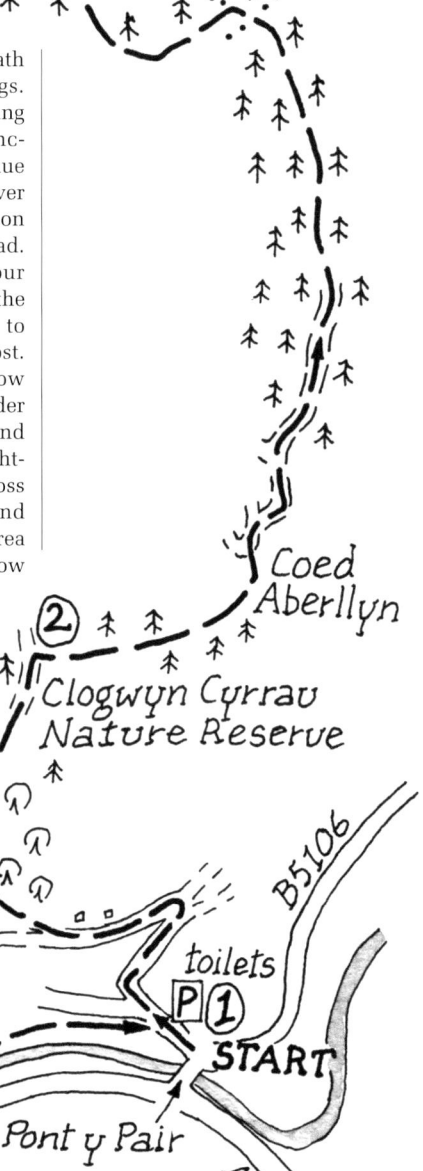

alongside the Afon Llugwy to reach a small picnic area. Follow the gravel path and boardwalk back to the car park at Pont y Pair.

the left hand ladder stile and follow the path steeply down to some old mine workings. Turn left at the junction with a track, keeping the workings to the right. At a track junction with a marker post on the left, continue ahead to another marker post and climb over the ladder stile on the left. Keep the fence on the left and go over a stile 100 yards ahead. Follow the path keeping the fence to your left. There is a short boggy section after the stile. Continue to and over the next stile to reach a track, where there is a marker post. Cross straight over at a marker post. Follow the wall on the right down and over a ladder stile. At the first the descent is very steep and rough, followed by much easier and delightful walking through mixed woodland. Cross a footbridge in front of a fine cataract and continue descending easily through an area of fine silver firs to a seat just before a narrow tarmac road.

4 Cross straight over the road and follow the path down to the slanting Miner's Bridge spanning the Afon Llugwy. Do not cross the bridge but keep the fence to the right and follow the path that closely follows the river. Although rough in parts this is a delightful walk. Go through a kissing gate and cross the meadow and through another kissing gate at the far side. Continue

WALK 6
HAFNA MINE & THE CONWY VALLEY VIEWPOINT

DESCRIPTION A pleasant 1½ mile walk taking in some very interesting mining history along the way. Following forest tracks for much of the walk care needs to be taken however on the descent of the steep steps through the mine workings. The view down the Conwy Valley is dramatic. Allow 45 minutes.

START At the Hafna Mine car park.

DIRECTIONS From Betws-y-Coed follow the B5106 to Gwydyr Castle. Turn left before the 'T' junction and drive up the road ignoring all turnings to the left and right to reach the Hafna Mine car park on the right.

From the car park walk up the forest track and around the barrier at a blue marker. Ignore the path on the right, where there is a red marker, for the Miner's path. Continue up the track to where a sign indicates the turn right to the viewpoint. There is a picnic table here. Return to the track and turn right. Continue to a three-way junction. Turn left and follow the track up and along past old mine workings to a fence on the left. Turn left by the electricity pole just beyond a marker post. Follow the track down past a marker post. At the next marker post 50 yards from the turn, bear right, with a fence on the left, down the path for 50 yards to a junction with a track. Go right down the track to where it bends right. On the left here is a stile. Climb over this and walk down steps into the ruins of Hafna Mine, There is a gated and locked entrance into an adit, as well as information boards highlighting the history. Descend to the car park.

There are records indicating that the mine was reworked in 1819 after Sir John Wynn, 1st Baronet, had taken samples around 1615. The reworking was undertaken by the then landowner Edward Lloyd from the Plas-yn-Cefn Estate. The mill complex was built in 1879 but work ceased in 1915.

Originally the mechanical processes were driven by a waterwheel but latterly replaced with a gas engine. Ore was brought into the mill via the now locked adit on the upper level, or the grilled, shaft to the left.

Hafna Mine is unique among all the mines in the Gwydyr Forest in that it had its own smelting house built in the 1880s. The furnace chimney, well seen from the lower levels, was sited away from the mill due to the toxic fumes. The line of the long flue can still be seen.

WALKS 6 & 7

WALK 7
DOUGLAS FIRS & ALL ABILITY PUZZLE TRAIL

DESCRIPTION A lovely ½ a mile stroll, (¾ of a mile for the extension), especially so on a summer evening, through mixed woodland. The animal puzzle trail is all-ability and pushchair friendly as well as being a great one for youngsters spotting and naming the 12 wildlife clues. The Douglas Firs are a magnificent sight alongside the tumbling Afon Llugwy. Allow 30 minutes to include spotting time.

START At the Pont y Pair car park in Betws-y-Coed.

DIRECTIONS From the A5 in Betws-y-Coed turn onto the B5106 that leads to Trefriw. Turn left immediately after crossing the bridge and then right into the car park. There is a small charge but there are toilets here.

The Douglas Firs were planted as young saplings in the 1920s. They now weigh over 10 tons each.

Cross the road from the car park and turn right to where the start of the walk will be found next to a finger post and information boards. Follow the gravel path onto a section of duckboards not far from the Afon Llugwy. At the 'Y' junction turn right and walk easily up to a track. Turn left along this for the all ability trail to where a gravel path can be followed to the left to reach a very fine picnic area close to the river. Follow the gravel path to the 'Y' path junction and bear right for the return walk to the car park.

A short extension can be made by the more able by crossing straight over the track mentioned above. Follow a zigzag path, with lots of seats at intervals, easily to where it joins the track. Cross straight over past a seat on the left along the gravel path as for the all ability trail. *Pont y Pair (the Bridge of the Cauldron) was designed and partially built by Howell the Mason from Bala who died around 1475. It was around this feature that the village grew. In spate the cauldron effect is obvious. Traffic often grinds to a halt here as scores of people stare at the waterfalls and crashing water from the bridge.*

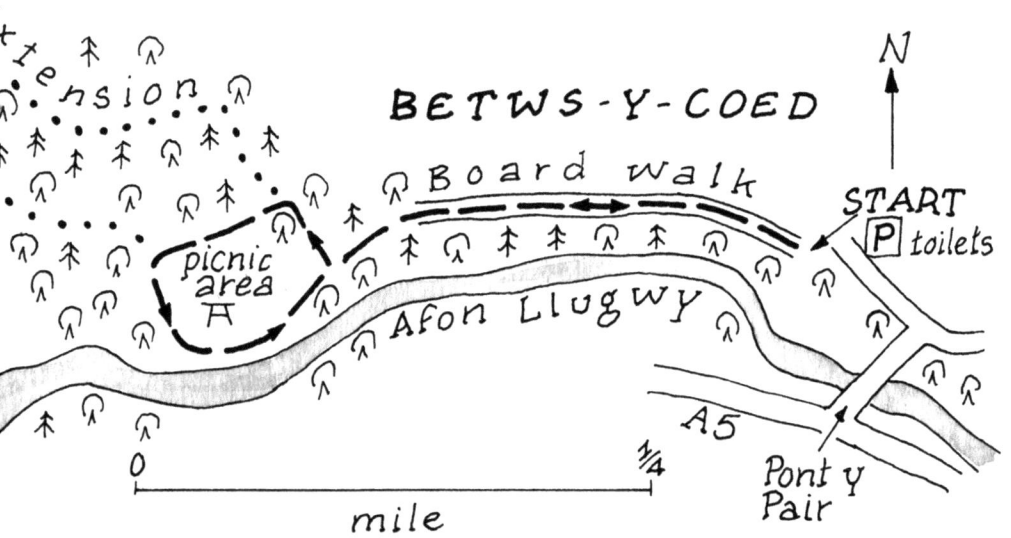

WALK 8
COED GARTHERYR & THE 'GHOST' VILLAGE OF RHIWDDOLION

DESCRIPTION This is a very fine walk of 6 miles through mixed woodland. Although the start, to reach Llyn Elsi is steep, the walk is then much easier being either level or downhill with very few rises. Paths are well defined. A visit to the abandoned mining village of Rhiwddolion is a must. Walking alongside the Afon Llugwy, at the end of the walk, having crossed the famed Miner's Bridge, is delightful. Allow 3½ hours.

START At the Pont y Pair car park in Betws-y-Coed.

DIRECTIONS From the A5 in Betws-y-Coed turn onto the B5106 that leads to Trefriw. Turn left immediately after crossing the bridge and then right almost immediately into the car park. There is a small charge but there are toilets here.

1 Turn left out of the car park and then right to walk over Pont y Pair. Beware of traffic on this narrow section. At the junction with the A5 turn left. Walk down the main street past the turning to the main car park and train station. Continue to where a large sign indicates Betws-y-Coed Motors. Turn right here, with Mairlys B&B is on the right, and walk up to the garage. Immediately beyond this and before the Vagabond Hostel, turn right. There is a very discreet waymark high up on the garage wall. Follow the path up and cross a footbridge. Continue steeply up the hill and cross another footbridge reaching a track 50 yards further. Turn left up this. Follow it to a large marker post by a standing stone and seat on the right. Turn right and cross the footbridge. Follow the zigzag path up the steep hillside past a white-topped post to reach a wall and continue to a track. Cross straight over. Follow the path to enter a clearing and a junction with the main forest road.

Cross straight over this and follow the gently rising path to reach the Ancaster Memorial overlooking Llyn Elsi. *The Ancaster memorial commemorates the Right Honourable Earl of Ancaster granting the right for a water supply to Betws-y-Coed Urban District Council on the 18th June 1914. There are fine views of Snowdonia from here with Moel Siabod being the nearer dominant mountain.*

2 Turn left down the path following it to join a forest road. Turn right down this and continue past the dam on the right to a marker post and obvious steep path going up to the right. Go right up this to a marker post on the left. Bear right on the obvious path and follow it to join a track. Continue straight ahead to where a marker post and five upright stones are reached on the right. Keep following the track (right is the footpath that continues the circuit around the lake). Ignore the next track on the right. Continue along the main track to pass between two wooden posts. Sometimes there is a pole barrier here. Continue to a 'Y' junction. Bear right and down still on the track, (there is a low cliff on the left a short way along), to the next barrier that is usually open. At the 'T' junction just beyond, turn up to the left following the track under the telephone and power lines. Ignore the track on the left with a barrier. Continue straight ahead to the access track to Pant-yr-Hyddod on the left at the top of the rise. This is immediately before the track starts to descend.

3 Turn left and go through the gate or over the ladder stile to the left. Follow the track past a marker post on the right to the next marker post where a path goes off to the right. Follow this as it rises above the low wall. Continue above the buildings to reach, and go through, a kissing gate. Follow the path directly opposite, firstly up then along following marker posts until a short descent reaches a fence with a marker post.

WALK 8

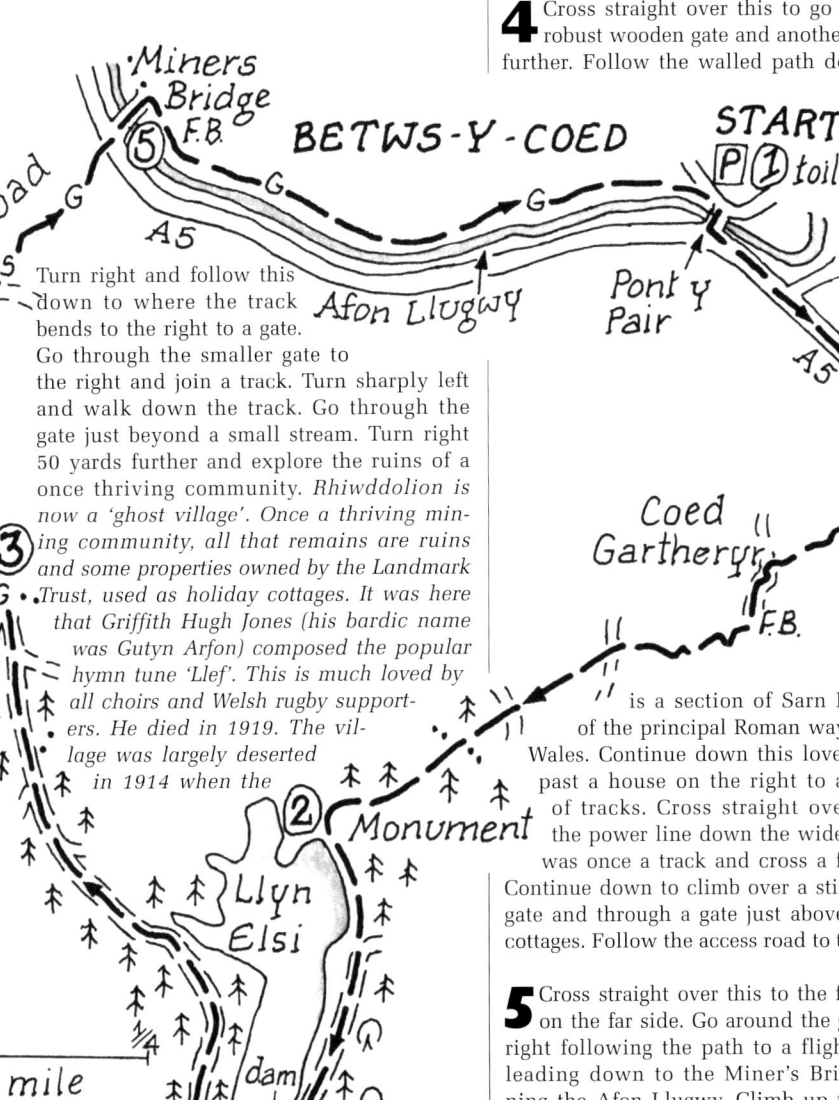

4 Cross straight over this to go through a robust wooden gate and another 15 yards further. Follow the walled path down. This

Turn right and follow this down to where the track bends to the right to a gate. Go through the smaller gate to the right and join a track. Turn sharply left and walk down the track. Go through the gate just beyond a small stream. Turn right 50 yards further and explore the ruins of a once thriving community. *Rhiwddolion is now a 'ghost village'. Once a thriving mining community, all that remains are ruins and some properties owned by the Landmark Trust, used as holiday cottages. It was here that Griffith Hugh Jones (his bardic name was Gutyn Arfon) composed the popular hymn tune 'Llef'. This is much loved by all choirs and Welsh rugby supporters. He died in 1919. The village was largely deserted in 1914 when the quarrying industry collapsed, and the last permanent inhabitant died there in 1974. The chapel was built in 1869 and closed in 1956.* Return to the small gate and keep following the track down to reach Ty Mawr. Continue down the narrow tarmac track to a major forest road junction.

is a section of Sarn Helen one of the principal Roman ways through Wales. Continue down this lovely section past a house on the right to a junction of tracks. Cross straight over. Follow the power line down the wide path that was once a track and cross a footbridge. Continue down to climb over a stile left of a gate and through a gate just above a line of cottages. Follow the access road to the A5.

5 Cross straight over this to the finger post on the far side. Go around the gate to the right following the path to a flight of steps leading down to the Miner's Bridge spanning the Afon Llugwy. Climb up this to the far side. Turn right and, keeping the fence to the right, follow the path that closely follows the river. Although rough in parts this is a delightful walk. Go through a kissing gate and cross the meadow and through another kissing gate at the far side. Continue alongside the Afon Llugwy to reach a small picnic area. Follow the gravel path and boardwalk back to the car park at Pont y Pair.

WALK 9
UP AND DOWN THE AFON LLUGWY

DESCRIPTION A lovely 1¾ mile stroll, especially so on a summer evening. Although the first part is alongside the busy A5 it does not detract from the splendour of the Afon Llugwy. This is an easy way to appreciate the broad leaved woodland by the side of the river and the huge Douglas Firs at the end of the walk. Allow an hour.

START At the Pont y Pair car park in Betws-y-Coed.

DIRECTIONS From the A5 in Betws-y-Coed turn onto the B5106 that leads to Trefriw. Turn left immediately after crossing the bridge and then right into the car park. There is a small charge but there are toilets here.

Turn left out of the car park. Turn right over Pont y Pair to the A5. Turn right along this and walk on the very wide pavement to reach Oakfield House seen on the opposite side of the road. Turn right over a stile located in the wall 50 yards past this where there is a footpath sign and immediately by the Betws-y-Coed sign. Follow the path over a footbridge to the steps leading down to the Miner's Bridge. Go down the steps and up over the bridge. Keeping the fence to the right, follow the path that closely follows the river. Although rough in parts this is a delightful walk. Go through a kissing gate and cross the meadow and through another kissing gate at the far side. Continue alongside the Afon Llugwy to reach a small picnic area. Follow the gravel path and boardwalk back to the car park at Pont y Pair.

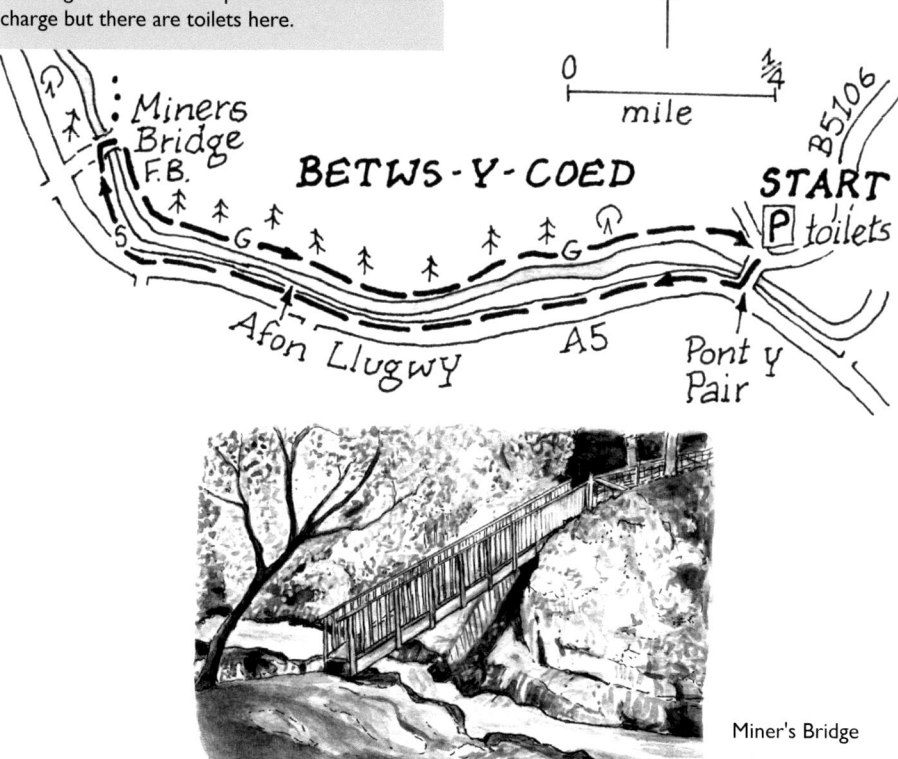

Miner's Bridge

WALKS 9 & 10

WALK 10
COED CAE HUDDYGL

DESCRIPTION Whichever way you decide to go round the return walk will be uphill! This lovely 2½ miles walk visits one of the most popular and very scenic waterfalls in Wales – Swallow Falls – without having to pay for the privilege. Allow 1½ hours although it is easy to take longer.

START At the Ty'n Llwyn car park.

DIRECTIONS From Betws-y-Coed follow the A5 towards Capel Curig. At Ty Hydd (the Ugly House) turn right and drive carefully up the very narrow minor road. The signed car park is ¾ mile along this on your right where there are some good views of the surrounding area. There are tables here for a picnic.

1 Walk past the picnic tables to the first of the yellow path marker posts. Follow the path into the wood and go past a large sign. Walk straight ahead down the path down the wide path passing marker posts at frequent intervals to join a wide track – *BEWARE of mountain bikers here*. Cross over diagonally to a marker post and continue down to a track at a 'Y' junction. Go left and down the right hand of side of the 'Y'. The track goes down almost reaching the Afon Llugwy. Keep on the track to where it becomes a path at marker post 18. At marker post 19 go down to the right to a fenced area where there are great but leafy views of the dramatic Swallow Falls.

2 Continue by the side of the fence on the right and rejoin the path. Follow it and descend to another viewpoint of the falls at marker post 20. Rejoin the path and turn right. Follow the fence on the right along the very fine high level path with dramatic views down into the gorge below. When the fence ends go left as indicated along a track. Go left again at a track junction and continue up to the next track junction. Turn right along the track and continue to a large sign on the right indicating the way back to the car park. Go left up the steps and follow a marked path through conifers to a right turn to reach a viewpoint. This gives magnificent views of Moel Siabod and Snowdon from the rocky summit. CARE is needed here as there is a rather long, vertical drop below you at this point. Return to the path and turn left on it. Continue up to the large sign seen on the outward walk. Turn right to return to the car park.

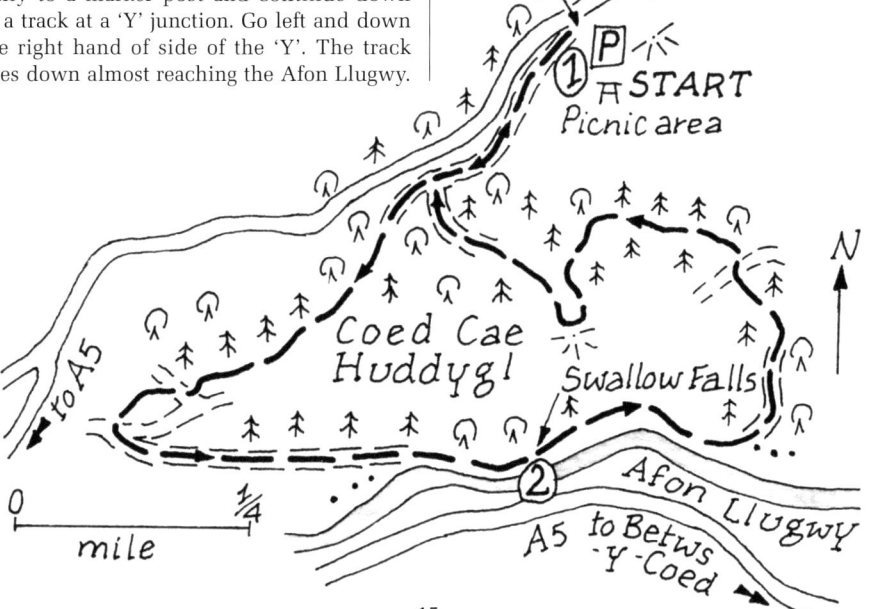

WALK 11
WOODLAND SCULPTURES AT LLYN MAIR

DESCRIPTION Although only ¾ mile this is a pleasant walk with much of interest packed in to it. Rushing streams, waterfalls, the Ffestiniog Railway, wood sculptures with easy to follow paths. This is one of Wales' last remaining rain forests and is home to wood mice, a host of birds including the pied flycatcher. Allow 45 minutes.

START At the car park belonging to the Countryside Council for Wales by the side of Llyn Mair.

DIRECTIONS From Porthmadog follow the A487 towards Maentwrog and Dolgellau. At the Oakeley Arms Hotel turn left on to the B4410 towards Rhyd. Continue for ¾ mile to the small car park on the right across from Llyn Mair.

Walk across the footbridge to the right and up the gravel path. IGNORE the steps on the right. *Part way up there is a wonderful carved double seat with backs of it shaped like oak leaves.* Continue up past a prominent way marker and through a gap to Tan y Bwlch station on the Ffestiniog Railway. *There is a café and toilets here.* Return to the gap and go down to the way marker. At the path junction turn left up the steps. At the top of these follow the obvious path down and across a footbridge. *Note the huge retaining wall of the railway to the left and the pretty stream issuing from the base of it.* Just beyond here the path splits at a 'Y' junction. Follow the right arm. Descend the clear path, with intermittent steps, that follows the left hand side of the pretty stream back to the car park. *Keep a lookout for carvings and sculptures on the way.*

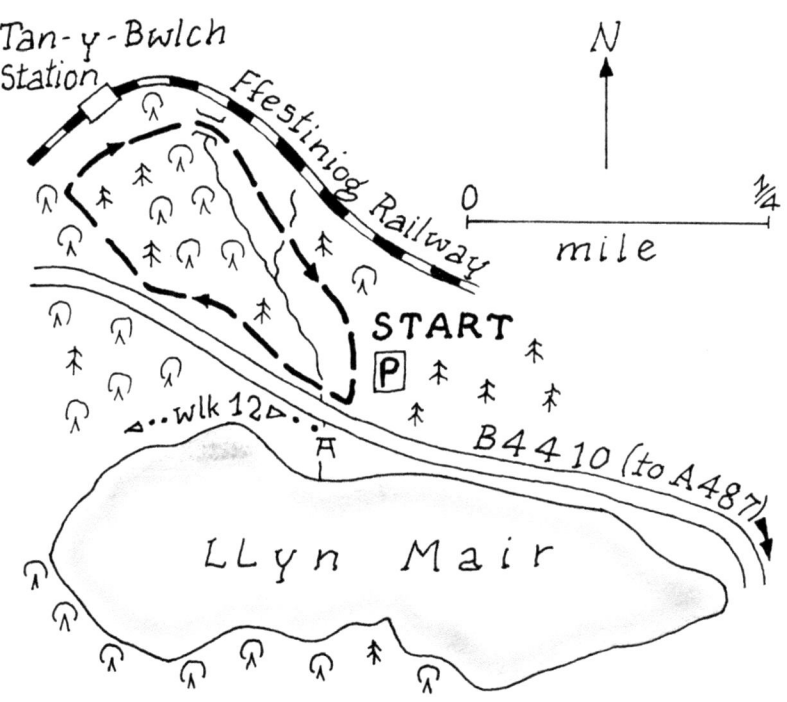

WALK 12
GIANT DOUGLAS FIRS AT TY'N Y GROES

DESCRIPTION This is a half-mile all ability trail which gives everyone a chance to see these magnificent trees. The path alongside the tumbling Afon Mawddach is delightful with many birds darting here and there. Although the trail can be completed in 20 minutes allow at least another 15 minutes sightseeing time.
START At the Forestry Commission car park Ty'n y Groes.
DIRECTIONS From Dolgellau follow the A470 towards Betws-y-Coed. Pass the Ty'n y Groes hotel on the left and turn right at the brown sign indicating Ty'n y Groes. The turning is also marked to Llanfachreth. Drive over the bridge crossing the Afon Mawddach and turn left immediately beyond it into the car park. There are toilets here.

Go out of the car park past the toilets and cross the road. Follow the gravel riverside path past picnic tables to an information panel. Continue along the path passingthrough enormous trees – the tallest in Coed y Brenin, 'The King's Guardians'. The path splits so follow the right arm alongside the river. There is an interesting 'viewing bed' just before the split where you can lie down on it and view the canopy high above.

The path continues close to the Mawddach giving good views of it to reach a seat with a crown! By this is the largest of all the trees here and has been named 'The King'. Continue to a path junction. This is where the all ability trail ends. Turn left to return to the car park on a loop.

However, with help it is possible to continue up to the tallest tree in the forest 'The Champion' and a viewing area of the river. Turn around here and retrace your way back to return to the car park. (For those who have strollers with toddlers on board the walk can be extended slightly from 'The Champion' by following yellow markers to the road and turning left down this back to the car park. Be CAREFUL as the road is narrow).

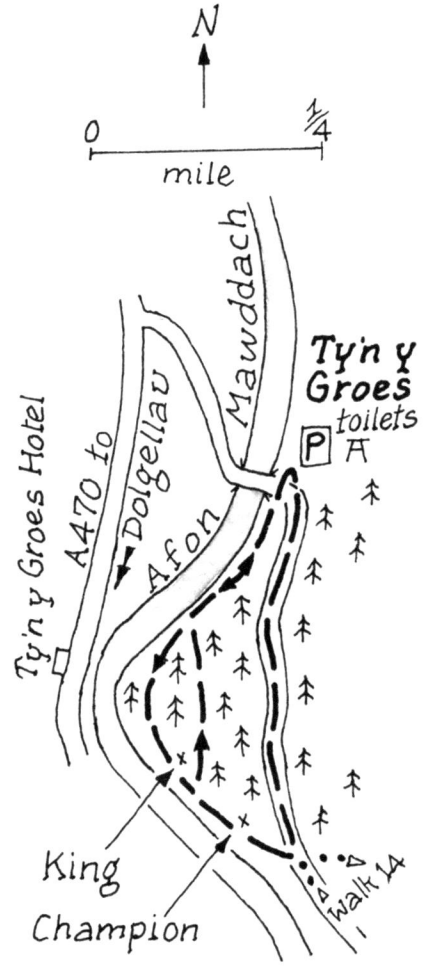

The Douglas Fir (Pseudotsuga Menziesii) *was discovered in 1791 in North America's Rocky Mountains by Archibald Menzies. The Scottish explorer, David Douglas sent the first seed back to Britain in 1827. The widest tree in the forest is known as 'The King' and measures 148 feet (45 metres) high, with a diameter of 39 inches (100cm) whilst the tallest is 'The Champion', at 161 feet (49 metres) with a diameter of 32 inches (80cm).*

WALK 13
COED LLYN MAIR & COED HAFOD Y LLYN

DESCRIPTION This is a lovely 2½ miles walk visiting two very pretty lakes. At a short section of cleared forest there are great views of the Moelwyns. If you time your walk to be at one of the railway crossings you will be met by the cheery waves from the driver and passengers enjoying the Ffestiniog Railway journey. Most of the walking is on forest tracks but with sections of paths that are easy to follow. Allow 1½ hours.

START At the car park belonging to the Countryside Council for Wales by the side of Llyn Mair.

DIRECTIONS From Porthmadog follow the A487 towards Maentwrog and Dolgellau. At the Oakeley Arms Hotel turn left on to the B4410 towards Rhyd. Continue for ¾ mile to the small car park on your right across from Llyn Mair.

1 Llyn Mair was created in 1889 and Llyn Hafod y Llyn around the same time. Just past point 11 is the millpond seen down to the left. Water from here supplied power for electricity generation for Plas Tan y Bwlch, the village of Maentwrog, as well as supplying power for the saw and flour mills. Leave the car park and carefully cross the road to the double gate. Go through this to reach a fine picnic site as well as entering the National Nature Reserve. Bear right past the tables along a track to a gap by the side of a gate. Beyond the gap follow the track to a junction atmarker post 26. Go left here and follow the wide path through a gap in the wall to enter Coed Hafod y Llyn. Keep on the path and cross a footbridge for the stream outlet from the fine pond above. Follow the path by the lake to a seat on the left. The path continues around the shore of the lake to point 10 where a track goes up to the right on concrete strips. Ignore this and continue alongside the lake, through a gap in a wall and up to another seat. Continue another 50 yards to point 11.

2 Turn acutely right and walk away from the lake. Continue up the track past a huge multi-limbed beech tree. 50 yards beyond this turn up right by a beech tree with twin trunks and up the path to the Ffestiniog Railway. Cross the line carefully looking out for trains. Walk up steps and through a gate. Bear right. Walk up to a house on the left and continue to a track junction. Go left and follow it to another track junction. (Straight ahead leads up to Hafod y Llyn). Turn left and continue past point 5 to point 6. Bear right through the cleared area on the right – *great views of the Moelwyns* – to point 7. Go left here to point 31 and continue along the track ignoring a turning right down to a white gate. At point 30, where there is a finger post on the right, keep following the track bearing left above the pretty Llyn Hafod y Llyn. Continue past a junction on the left to another finger post. This one is to the left. Keep on the track and walk down to point 16. Continue to a seat just up on the right. *These woodlands are very special and are of European importance. They are a designated Special Area for Conservation (SAC) because of the large extent of oak woodland with the damp habitat providing ideal conditions for mosses, ferns, liverworts and lichens. Hundreds of species can be found in the area. The rare Lesser Horseshoe Bat has its European stronghold here. Oak was commercially grown here for the ship building industry that thrived in the 18th and 19thC. Conifers were also grown for the local slate industry which was the man source of income for the Oakeley family of Plas Tan y Bwlch. Birdlife is plentiful with spring and summer being extremely good for spotting pied flycatchers, redstarts and wood warblers among the more familiar birds. In winter the lakes are a big magnet for ducks. Other rarer birds have been noted here – nightjars, goshawks and ospreys.*

3 Turn right 20 yards beyond this down a good path and pass a picnic table. Continue following the gentle path as it meanders lazily to the dam. Cross this and walk up to the finger post at point 30. Turn left along the track, then left again 50 yards

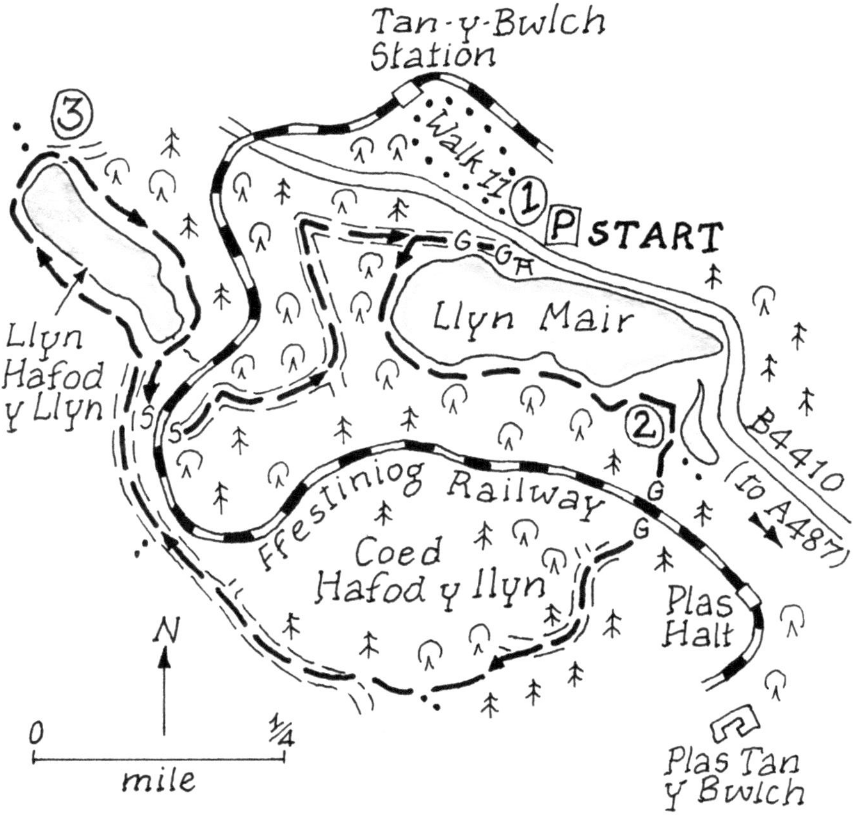

WALK 13

further on and descend to the white gate seen previously. Looking out for trains, climb over the stile. Carefully cross the line and over the stile at the far side. Walk down the track passing point 28 and continue to point 27. At the track junction here go to the left and walk along to a gate. This is bypassed by walking to the right of it. Continue down the track to point 26 and familiar ground. Go straight ahead back to the car park.

Llyn Mair

WALK 14
MYNYDD PENRHOS & THE DOUGLAS FIRS OF COED Y BRENIN

DESCRIPTION This 3 mile walk extends walk 12 through the magnificent trees. It crosses the road and starts a quite long uphill walk through mixed woodland to the summit of Mynydd Penrhos. Magnificent views are to be had close by another ornate seat. The well marked path follows green markers. Allow 2 hours for completion.

START At the Forestry Commission car park Ty'n y Groes.

DIRECTIONS From Dolgellau follow the A470 towards Betws-y-Coed. Pass the Ty'n y Groes hotel on the left and turn right at the brown sign indicating Ty'n y Groes. The turning is also marked to Llanfachreth. Drive over the bridge crossing the Afon Mawddach and turn left immediately beyond it into the car park. There are toilets here.

1 Go out of the car park past the toilets and cross the road. Follow the gravel river side path past picnic tables to an information panel. Continue along the path that goes through enormous trees – *the tallest in Coed y Brenin*. These trees at the start have been dubbed 'The King's Guardians'. The path splits so follow the right arm alongside the river. *There is an interesting 'viewing bed' just before the split where you can lay down and view the canopy high above.* The path continues close to the Mawddach giving good views of it to reach a seat with a crown! *By this seat is the largest of all the trees here and has been named 'The King'.* Continue to a path junction. Continue up past 'The Champion' and a viewing area of the river. Continue on the gravel path to the road.

2 Cross straight over and follow the path uphill to a junction with a bike track – SO TAKE CARE. Walk straight ahead to a post with a green arrow and bear left up the path. This climbs steadily and up some steps. Continue up to a slightly steeper section. Bear left at the next marker post and up to reach mixed woodland. The path levels here before rising again beyond a hurdle by a marker post. At the next marker post bear right up three steps from where a quite steep ascent leads to a grassy belvedere, where there is a cairn. The superb views from here are extensive – *Y Garn and the Rhinogs in front and to the right Snowdon can be seen in the far distance. To the left is Cadair Idris*. A short gradual ascent leads, past a seat, to the true summit of Mynydd Penrhos where there are views eastwards towards the Arans and Rhobell Fawr.

3 The path descends into the forest and through a broken wall. It continues gradually down through a hurdle to a marker post. Turn right as indicated along the track. Ignore the path on the left by a yellow topped pole. Continue along the track to where it ends in a small turning area where there is a marker post. A grassy path descends fairly steeply and through another hurdle. Continue down, *with good views of Cadair Idris in front of you*, to enter the forest of Douglas Firs. Pass through another hurdle to reach a track. Turn right up this, ignoring the obvious signed path on the far side of the track, and continue for 200 yards to a marker post.

4 Turn left here and down past another marker post almost immediately. Continue to where the path descends to a bike track at a marker post, so again TAKE CARE. (Red = Red Dragon track and Black = Beast track). Turn right, keeping a watchful eye for cyclists, to reach a 'Y' junction. The bike route goes up to the right. Turn left at a marker post, following the path to reach the road. Turn right up this for 50 yards and turn left. Follow the path close to the river before it rises slightly reach the gravel path of the outward walk. Turn left along it back to the car park.

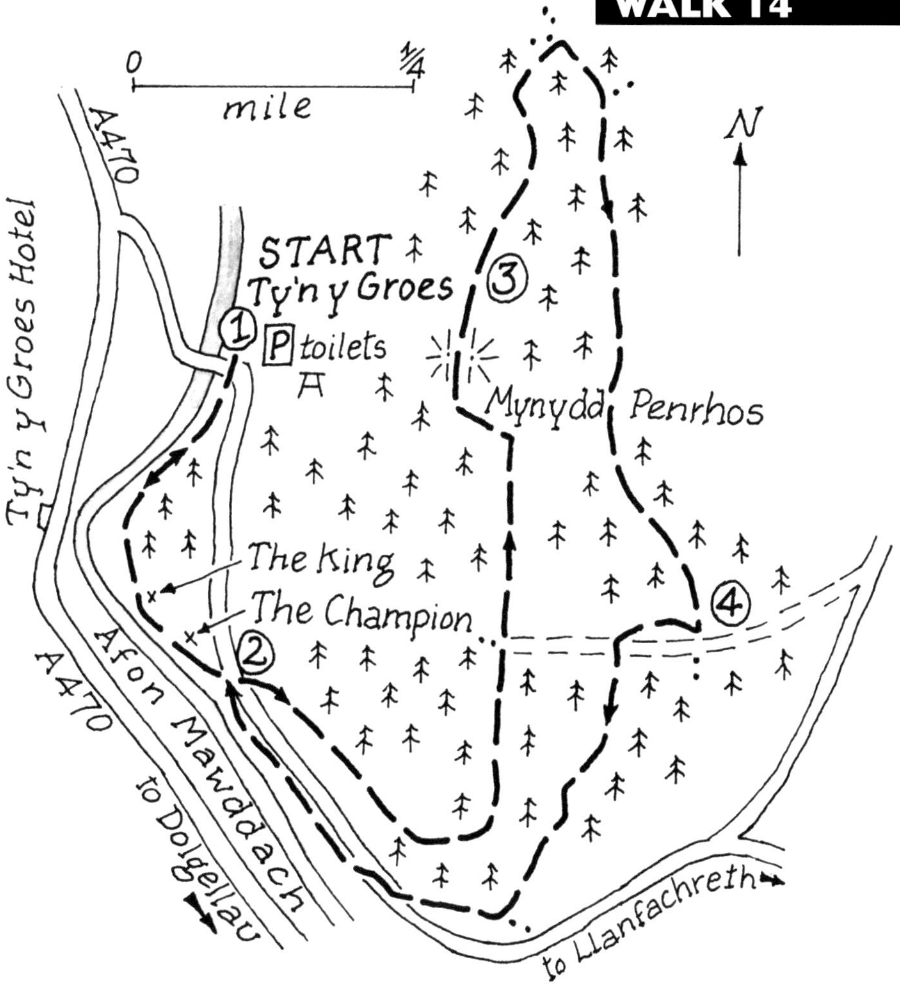

WALK 14

Coed y Brenin

WALK 15
WOODLAND WAY TO TY MAWR

DESCRIPTION This is a very fine 6¼ miles walk and initially follows the dramatic Afon Lledr through fine woodland. A steep climb then leads to the wonderfully sited Ty Mawr. A long ascent from here starts the return walk to Dolwyddelan. There are superb views of Moel Siabod on the way as well as the surrounding countryside. In all but the driest weather the section across an open area is very boggy as is the descent through the forest. The final section goes along a track back into the village. Allow 3¾ hours.

START From the railway station at Dolwyddelan.

DIRECTIONS From Betws-y-Coed follow the A5 towards Llangollen. Cross the Waterloo Bridge and turn right on to the A470. This is followed to Dolwyddelan. Turn left opposite Y Gwydyr Hotel. There is also a Spar shop on the corner. Continue to the railway station. If coming from the south turn right off the A470 opposite Y Gwydyr and continue to the railway station. There is a voluntary pay-and-display car park here.

1 Walk out of the car park and turn immediately right along a narrow road with the school on the left. Continue along the lane and go through a gate just before Ty Isaf Farm. Pass through three more gates in the farmyard. Ignore the track on the right and continue through another gate and follow the track alongside the Afon Lledr. Note the fine footbridge on the left. At the finger post go straight ahead. Ignore the path over the bridge. Continue and pass through a rickety metal gate. Walk to the left of some cottages on a grassy track. Keep going along this, often flooded in wet weather. Pass under the railway line. Bear up to the left and through a gate. Follow the better track and pass a marker post. Descend to a good track and go through a white gate to join a narrow tarmac road.

2 Follow this and pass Pont y Pant railway station. Continue to a wider road ignoring a path to the right. Keep walking along the road and bear right at the sign for Lledr Hall and go up past Plas Hall Hotel. The road descends and bears right into a parking area for Lledr Hall Outdoor Centre. Take the small path ahead at the bend and pass to the right of metal railings. Cross the access road to the centre. Go through a metal gate and across a footbridge. Bear left along the path to the river. Follow this path, *which will be impassable when the river is in flood*, to where it becomes walled. Continue alongside the river with some lovely views. Go through a gate, waymark, and another 200 yards further, waymark. Turn sharp left immediately after this and follow the often boggy path above a superb gorge. Cross over a low section of wall and continue, to emerge from the woodland at a ladder stile. Cross this and continue following the riverside path before going up to go through a gate to join a good track at Tanaeldroch Farm where a finger post indicates the way to Penmachno.

3 Bear right and through the gate just below the farm. The steep grassy track climbs up to cross a ladder stile just before going under the railway. Continue up to reach a main forest road. Cross this diagonally to the left and take the less well defined track on the right. Follow this up, steeply at first, then less so before it descends to a gate. Go through this to reach a narrow road. Turn right up this and follow it passing 'Cyfyng',

WALK 15

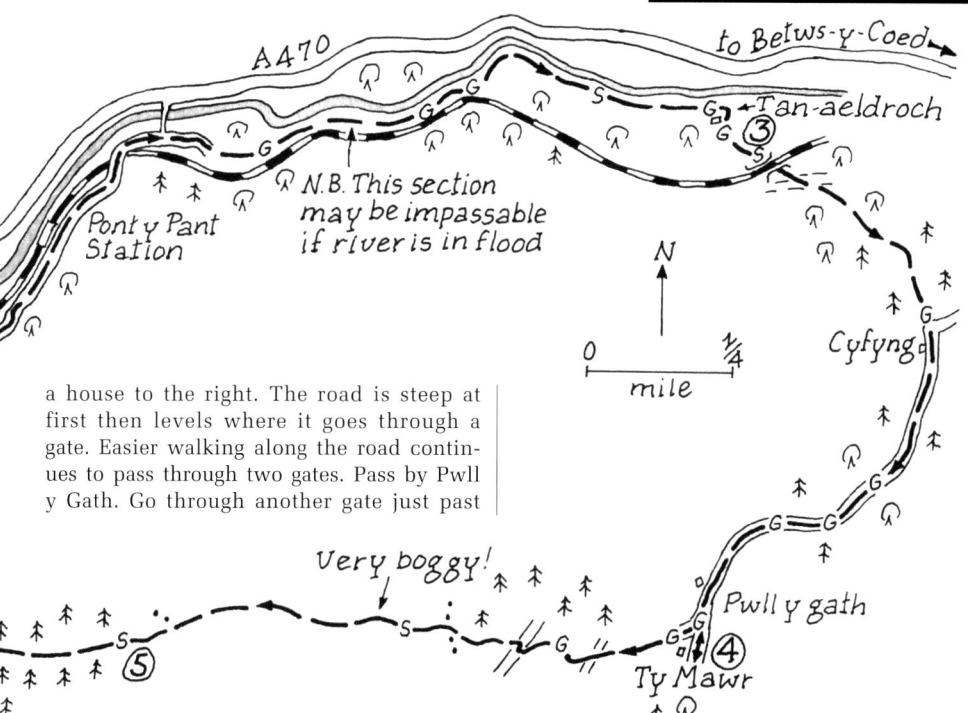

a house to the right. The road is steep at first then levels where it goes through a gate. Easier walking along the road continues to pass through two gates. Pass by Pwll y Gath. Go through another gate just past this and continue to Ty Mawr. (*Open April to October*). Bishop William Morgan was born at Ty Mawr Wybrnant. He studied at Cambridge and became ordained as a deacon in the Church of England. He was the vicar of Llanrhaeadr-ym-Mochnant and Archbishop of St Asaph in 1601. However, his greatest contribution was his translation of the bible into Welsh. Not only did this enable people to worship in their own language, it also safeguarded the future of the Welsh language. The house is now owned by the National Trust and a fee is payable for a look inside.

4 Return through the gate and turn left 10 yards further at a marker post. Follow the path up and through another gate 60 yards further on. Bear left up the hill and pass a marker post confirming the way ahead. The path continues between walls and goes through a gate. Continue up to join a forest road. Go right for 5 yards then turn left at the marker post and sign for Dolwyddelan. Follow the path up to another forest road, marker post. Cross over and climb the seemingly never ending path to climb over a dilapidated ladder stile *with care*, to reach open land. The path rises gently to a sudden and fine view of Moel Siabod. The next 1000 yards are extremely boggy. Squelch across this to reach a stile, waymark.

5 Cross this to enter a coniferous forest. Follow the path down, still quite boggy to a forest road. Cross straight over this and follow the still boggy path to a marker post on the left. Turn left as indicated. Follow the path to a fence. Keeping this to the right continue to where it turns at 90 degrees to the right, with a marker post on the left. Continue ahead following the path through the forest passing over the top of what appears to be a rather large quarry. After a short steep descent pass between the walls of a ruined winding house. Descend the steep incline to reach a track. Turn left. Go through a gate and follow the track to a four-way junction. Go straight ahead through a kissing gate and follow the track down to a tarmac road. Follow this down to reach the car park.

WALK 16
CAE GWIAN & MAWDDACH ESTUARY VIEW

DESCRIPTION This 1½ mile walk has some lovely views from the high ground over the Mawddach Estuary. The broadleaf woodland has a predominance of birch trees. Allow 45 minutes.

START At the Tilhill Forestry car parking area for Cae Gwian.

DIRECTIONS From Dolgellau follow the A470 towards Betws-y-Coed. At the roundabout in Llanelltyd turn left towards Barmouth on the A496. Follow this road for 5 miles until a sharp right hand turn can be made on to a very minor road. It is difficult to spot this single track road. Drive up this steep, narrow road for ½ mile to the car parking area on the left. The entrance is marked by a huge upstanding block of stone. There is a small but pretty pond overlooked by a seat.

Follow the forest road away from the entrance and walk around the barrier. Turn left 200 yards further on an overgrown track. Follow this up to where it becomes a path. This continues below a summit and becomes boggy before reaching a short steep section. Go up this gravelly/stony path to the left with increasingly lovely views of the Rhinogs to the right. The path becomes level and reaches a vague junction. Go up to the right to appreciate further the fine view of the surrounding countryside to the west. Return to the junction and go right along a narrow faint path through low birch trees. Pass by a seat on the left and continue down

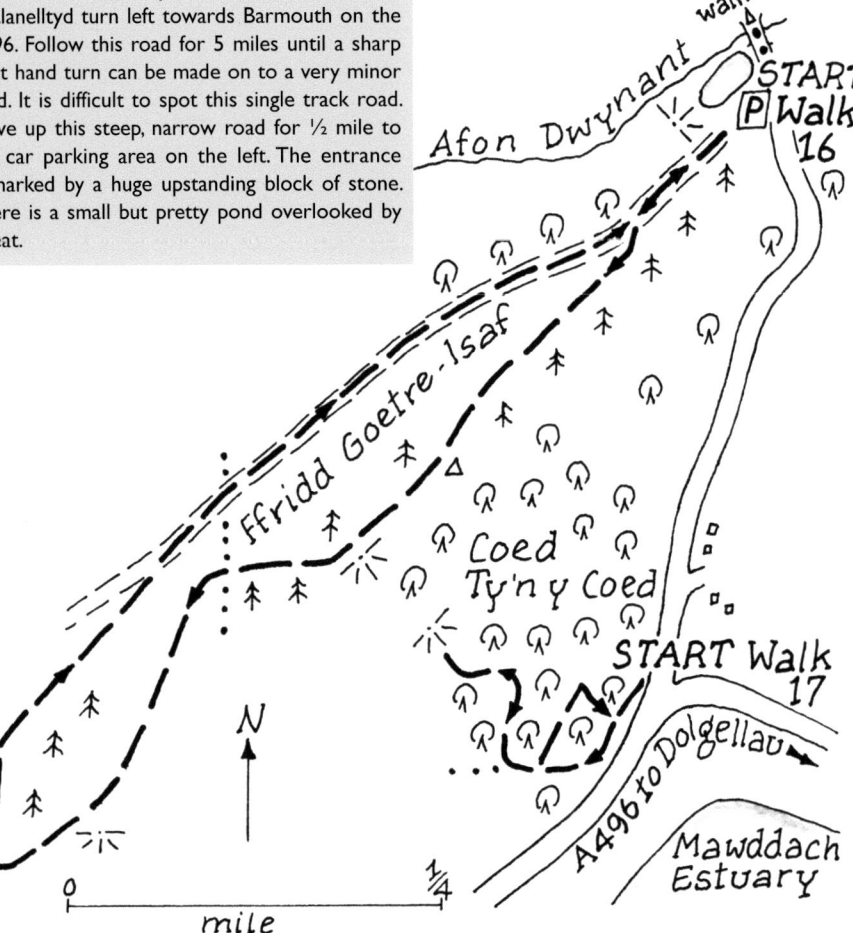

WALKS 16 & 17

– *with views of the Mawddach Estuary filtering through the trees. Just before the steep descent there is a superb view of Barmouth Bridge and the Mawddach Estuary.* Descend the steep path as it curves to the right to join a grassy track and power line pole. Turn right and follow the track to join the forest road which is followed to the right back to your car.

WALK 17
COED TY'N Y COED

DESCRIPTION This 1¼ mile walk has some truly exceptional views from the high point towards Cadair Idris as well as to the Mawddach Estuary. The outward walk is all uphill and is quite steep but that means it is all downhill on the way back! The woodland itself is beautiful and many sessile oaks display their characteristic contorted branches. Birch is the predominant tree found here. Allow 45 minutes or longer depending how long you absorb the view. The wood is managed by the Woodland Trust.

START At the large lay-by just after turning onto the dead end road.

DIRECTIONS From Dolgellau follow the A470 towards Betws-y-Coed. At the roundabout in Llanelltyd turn left towards Barmouth on the A496. Follow this road for 5 miles until a sharp right hand turn can be made on to a very minor road. It is difficult to spot this single track road. Drive up the road for 50 yards to the large pull in on the left and park here but please do not block access to the gate.

Walk around the right hand side of the gate to the information board. Follow the track up. Ignore the path on the right but 20 yards ahead there is a ground level barrier of logs. Turn up to the right here and follow the steep zigzag path up to join a better defined one. Turn left up this. Pass by a rustic seat on the left close to a wall and continue up another 15 yards. Turn right where there is a Woodland Trust sign indicating Coed Cadw. The path continues zigzagging steeply up to reach a wall. Go right into the thinning wood and reach clear ground above the trees. *As height is gained tremendous views open up.* The walk ends at a seat where the views are truly spectacular. Drink in the splendour before returning and following the main path all the way back to the lay-by.

Sessile Oak (Quercus Petraea) has been designated the national tree of Wales. 'Petraea' means 'of rocky places.'

From the car park return to the road and turn left along it for ¼ mile. Turn sharply to the right up the narrow dead-end road signed Cae Gwian to a footpath sign on the left. Walk up the track from the end of the tarmac. At a track junction bear left. Follow the track up ignoring another track junction on the right. Continue steadily uphill until an information board is reached on the left. Continue on the track and around the edge of the forest of mature conifers. At the top of the track there is a great view of the Cadair Idris range ahead and Y Figra to the left. The track continues down and enters mature conifers.

Just after this the track bends sharply to the left and slightly up before going downhill where it shrinks to a path. Follow this pleasant path down where there are glimpses of the Rhinogs, Y Figra and Cadair Idris through the trees to emerge on a forest track. Turn right and follow the outward walk back to the car park.

WALK 18

CAE GWIAN & CADAIR IDRIS VIEW

DESCRIPTION This 2½ mile walk has some lovely views from the high ground towards Cadair Idris as well as to the Rhinogs. The majority of the walk follows tracks. Allow 1½ hours.

START At the Tilhill Forestry car parking area for Cae Gwian.

DIRECTIONS From Dolgellau follow the A470 towards Betws-y-Coed. At the roundabout in Llanelltyd turn left towards Barmouth on the A496. Follow this road for 5 miles until a sharp right hand turn can be made on to a very minor road. It is difficult to spot this single track road. Drive up this steep, narrow road for ½ mile to the car parking area on the left. The entrance is marked by a huge upstanding block of stone. There is a small but pretty pond overlooked by a seat.

Cae Gwian covers an area of 192 hectares and is of mixed forest. Only 7% is un-forested. Managed by Tilhill there are broadleaf trees, conifers, such as Sitka Spruce, Pine, Fir, Larch and Western Hemlock, saplings, high forest and open moorland. This is a working forest combining both timber 'farming', conservation with walking routes. There are no waymarks here! Most of the timber matures after 50 years and produces 450 cubic metres of timber from each hectare. The nearby Cae Gwian mine produced a small quantity of gold in the 19thC.

WALKS 18 & 19

WALK 19
TAN Y COED & COED CWMCADIAN

DESCRIPTION This is a lovely 1½ mile walk through mixed woodland. It has the added attraction of a pretty waterfall and stream. Walking time is an hour but allow 1½ hours or longer if having a picnic at one of the many available sites.

START At the Forestry Commission car park for Tan y Coed.

DIRECTIONS From Machynlleth follow the A487 towards Dolgellau until signs indicate the Tan y Coed car park. Turn left into this where there are toilets, information board and leaflets.

The Forestry Commission commenced the tree planting here just after the First World War because the war effort had used up much of Britain's timber. This process continued through the Second World War with help from the Land Army Girls. They were known as 'Timber Jills'. A great deal of the work was undertaken by hand with horses being used to haul out the logs.

1 Leave the car park by the fine, carved fir cone. Walk up the steps and follow the path past picnic tables to where a marker post indicates the red and green walk. (This walk follows the green). Walk gradually up the path to a junction. Here the red walk goes straight ahead. Turn right and walk steeply up the hill via several switchbacks through conifers to where the path eases. The path swings left and continues above the conifers through varied deciduous trees – *beech and sycamore are predominant*. Continue to a marker post immediately before a track. Turn left and walk past an information board to the left and a wooden seat to the right. The path descends gradually at first and then becomes steep to reach a path junction. (This is where the red route joins and continues as in 2 below).

2 Continue more gently down to join a track at a marker post. Cross straight over to another marker post and turn right as indicated to pass by an information board to the left and picnic table to the right. Keep following the path as it descends gently to join the lovely tumbling Nant Cwmcadian. Follow the stream-side path through a narrow rock cutting. Immediately beyond this there is a good view down to the fine water chute below a small but pretty waterfall. Keep following the stream-side path which, unfortunately, swings away from it all too quickly. Ascend through the wood to reach a junction with a marker post. Turn right up the steps to the next marker by the junction of a main forest track. Go right down this to return to the car park.

The red route is an easier version of the above and is no less attractive as it misses out the steep climb when the green route turns right. It continues straight ahead from the junction ascending gradually to point 2 above. This is known as the Cwm Cadian Trail as well as the Animal Puzzle Trail, a great walk for the whole family. The leaflet gives you clues to find the hidden animals!

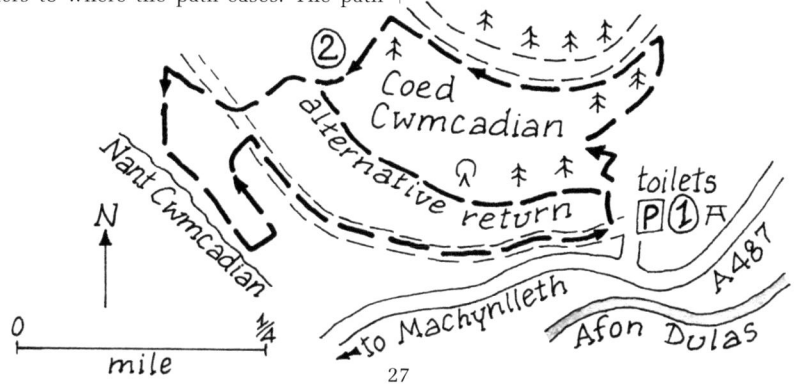

WALK 20
COED CORS Y GEDOL

DESCRIPTION This is a superb 2½ mile walk through beautiful natural woodlands enhanced by a lively stream. It also visits Pont Fadog, a fine bridge built in 1762 as well as a visit to a Neolithic burial chamber. Allow 2 hours.
START From the car park in Tal-y-Bont by the toilets.
DIRECTIONS From Barmouth follow the A496 north towards Harlech. Drive over the bridge on entering the village of Tal-y-Bont and turn right into the car park.

1 From the information board in the car park follow the path alongside the Afon Ysgethin. Continue past the Ysgethin Inn and walk to the right of a small stone building. Follow the path up on the left hand side of the river to a stile to the right of a gate. Climb over the stile and continue to ascend a flight of steps that take you high above the river. At the path junction turn right and pass the seat seen ahead. A level wide path continues alongside the river to where it rises gently to another junction. Bear right, still following the delightful river. Continue to a gate. Go through this and follow the gently rising path to join a tarmac road and way mark in front of Llety Lloegr. Turn right here and walk down the road to pass through a gate onto Pont Fadog. Return to where you emerged on to the road at Llety Lloegr.

2 Continue up the very quiet and narrow road. After a ¼ mile there is a very fine Neolithic burial chamber on the left. *This Neolithic burial chamber, one of a number in the area, dates back almost 5000 years. They were originally covered by a mound of stones or earth. Unfortunately 'robbers' left the chambers exposed in the state you see them today but highlighting the fine example of early construction.* Continue along the road – *with lovely views of the sea in front and the Rhinogs behind.* After another ¼ mile go through a gate and turn left down the tarmac road to a sharp left hand bend. Keep following the tarmac road to a 'T' junction ignoring the track to the right that leads down to Cors-y-Gedol. *Cors-y-Gedol literally means the 'bog of hospitality'. This may sound strange nowadays but several centuries ago the surrounding area was very marshy and may account for the rather odd title. Cors-y-gedol was the home of the Vaughan family until 1791 when the family died out. They were one of the main families in the area and were descendents of Osborn Fitzgerald an Irishman who settled here in the 13thC. The Vaughans were well respected and prominent in Meirioneth affairs serving as MPs, High Sheriffs and Magistrates. The Mostyns, another aristocratic family, having been passed the estate, lived here until 1860 after the Vaughans. The present building dates back to 1576 but has undergone much alteration and additions since then.* Turn left at the 'T' junction and continue down the 'leafy' road to a lay-by on the right. Opposite this is a gate.

3 Go left through it and follow the level wide path to a gate. Go through this and turn right 5 yards beyond down a narrow path. Continue through the fine wood to a stile on your right. DO NOT cross this but bear left and follow the fence. Cross a tiny footbridge over a stream and keep following the fence. At the four way junction where the fence bends right follow the fence line to the fence corner just before another tiny footbridge at a path junction. Walk straight ahead at first following a tiny stream down to a wall. Follow this to where it ends and drop down to the stream below on the right. Continue down to a main path. Turn right here and follow it down and through an old metal gate. Continue to a narrow tarmac road. Follow this down to a larger road. Turn left and return to the car park.

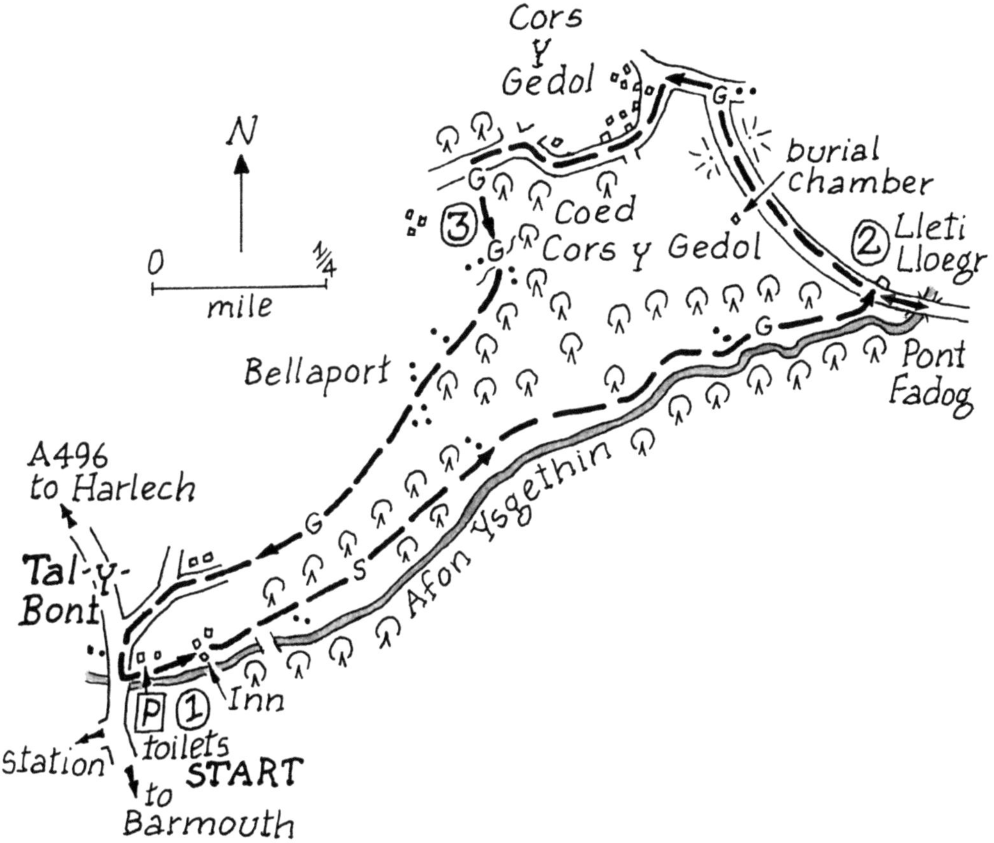
Cors
Y
Gedol
N
0
1/4
mile
burial
chamber
Coed
Cors y Gedol
3
2
Lleti
Lloegr
Bellaport
Pont
Fadog
A496
to Harlech
Afon Ysgethin
Tal-y-
Bont
Inn
P
1
toilets
START
Station
to
Barmouth

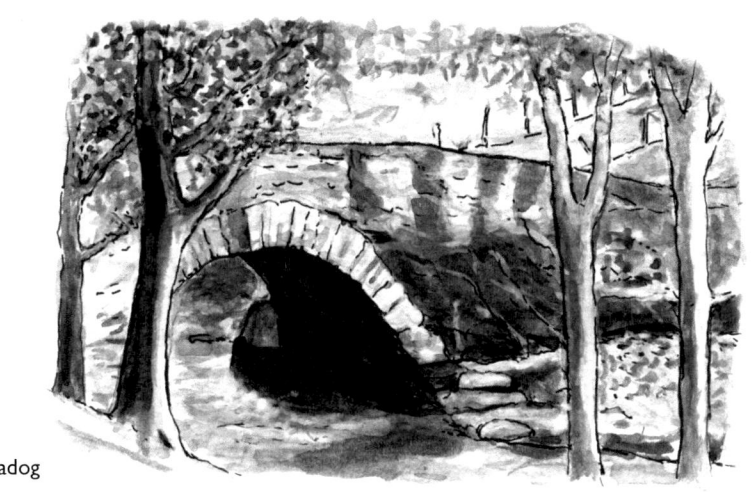

Pont Fadog

WALK 21
AFON ARAN & COED CROES

DESCRIPTION A pleasant 3½ mile walk based on the Afon Aran. Water is never very far away but is elusive at times. The walk takes you high into the woodland, close to the foothills of Cadair Idris, above Dolgellau. There are some fine views. Allow 2¼ hours.

START From the leisure centre car park in Dolgellau.

1 Turn right from the car park entrance and into the supermarket car park. Walk through this and turn right to the road bridge over the Afon Aran but do not go over it. Cross the road and follow the access road on the left of the river to the right. Carry on up the road until there is a choice of ways. Do not take the footpath signed to the left but take the narrow, steep uphill road to the right. Pass two houses on the way. When the tarmac ends, and a track continues, turn right on to a path that leads into Coed Abereint. Follow this narrow grassy path with glimpses of waterfalls below to the right on the Afon Aran. This path joins a much more defined one which continues down to a pretty waterfall.

2 Cross the footbridge and walk through some ruins. Continue to a narrow tarmac road. Cross the bridge and bear left through a waymarked triangular fence slot. Walk up to another waymark and turn left. Follow the path to the right of a fence to the remains of a fulling mill, one of many used in the area for the woollen industry. There are the remains of a leat here. The path becomes steep from here and joins up with a fence. Keep this to your left – *fine cataracts below at this point* – and continue. Pass through a plantation of cypresses to a stile. Go over this and subsequent stepping stones in the stream. Continue following the path to reach another stream and footbridge. Cross the bridge and follow the path above a boarded up building to emerge on a narrow tarmac road close to a house, Frongoch.

3 Turn right uphill. Follow the road with the rushing waters of the Afon Aran below. Climb steadily to reach a junction. Turn left here, signed to Dref Cerrig, and through a gate. Continue to a road junction and go straight ahead up the road to another gate in 500 yards. Go through this and continue for another 60 yards to a waymark on the right. Turn sharply right here and follow the clear path. Cross a small stream and after passing through a gap in a substantial wall there are the ruins of an old farmhouse on the left. Keep following the path to emerge at a narrow tarmac road. *The building on the left was an old school c1882 and is now a private house.*

4 Turn left, then right 10 yards further on, through a gate signed Pandy Gader. Cross to the field below the house to a footbridge over the Afon Aran. Cross this and turn right along a track. Ignore the footpath sign on the left after 60 yards and continue down the track. Where it goes through a substantial wall turn immediately left where there is a yellow marker post. Cross the stile and continue 20 yards alongside the wall until and bear half right by a large mossy boulder. Follow a path that keeps close to the wall on the left. Where the wall bends left go straight ahead at a waymark and follow another wall on the left. Keep following the

WALK 21

wall to another waymark. Go straight ahead past it and down to double stiles. The first is a crude log affair over the fence followed by steps down the far side of the wall to reach a track. Turn right and follow the track to a narrow tarmac road.

5 Turn left and walk past Parc Cottage. *This was once the home of Cadwaladr Jones, the last person to be hanged in Dolgellau in 1877. He had confessed to the murder of a young local woman.* Keep following the road to a gate just before the next house, Esgeiriau. Do not go through the gate, but turn right down a way marked path following a stream on the left to a gate above three steps. Go through the gate and down through the wood to join a much wider, though steeper path which is followed down to the bridge you passed at the start of section 2. Turn left and follow the narrow road back into town to arrive in Eldon Square. Go right along the main street back to the car park.

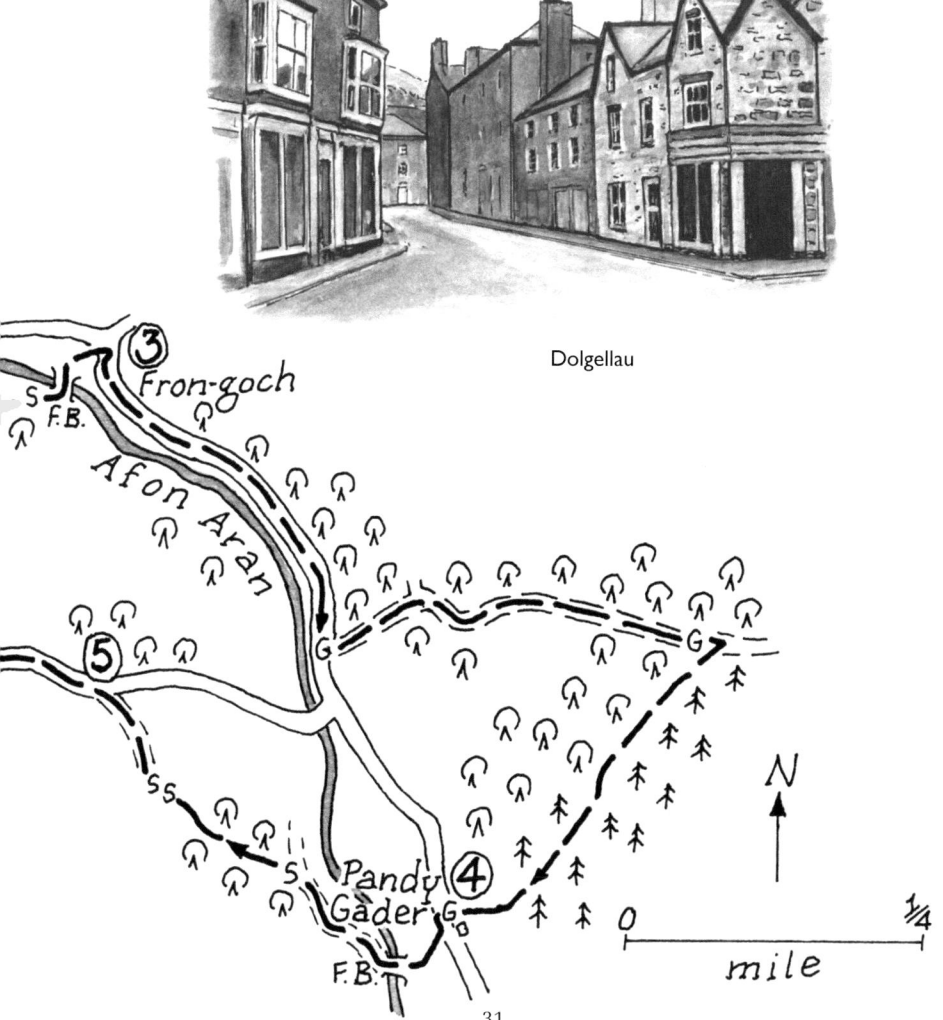

Dolgellau

WALK 22
COED Y CWM

DESCRIPTION A pleasant 1¼ mile walk through mixed woodland in this nature reserve. The spring flowers are a joy to see, Bluebells, Wild Garlic and the rare Bird's-nest and Blue-eyed Mary Orchids, along with many others, are all found here. Allow 45 minutes.
START From the large lay-by on the B4572.
DIRECTIONS From Aberystwyth follow the A487 towards Machynlleth. At the top of the hill turn left onto the B4572. The turning for Waunfawr is to the right. Continue along the B4572 for ¾ mile to the lay-by. From Machynlleth it is easiest to drive to Aberyswyth and turn right onto the B4572 at the top of the hill leading down into town.

1 The lay-by has an information board and a stream flows underneath. Take the path on the left hand side of the pull in and climb a flight of steps. When these end follow the path up almost to the top of the wood. Bear right and slightly down to cross a footbridge spanning the small stream. The path descends gradually to a waymarked junction with a track.

2 Cross straight over and follow the permissive path through delightful woodland to a low marker post on the left. Bear right and down passing a seat to the left, on the way to reaching a junction with a wide path, where there is waymark on a tree. Take the right hand path of two and continue along this to the B4572.

3 Turn sharp right up the track to a marker post on the left. Turn left and pass a heart shaped trunk with a marker. Continue gradually up to a seat. The path now descends and becomes quite steep as the lay-by is reached.

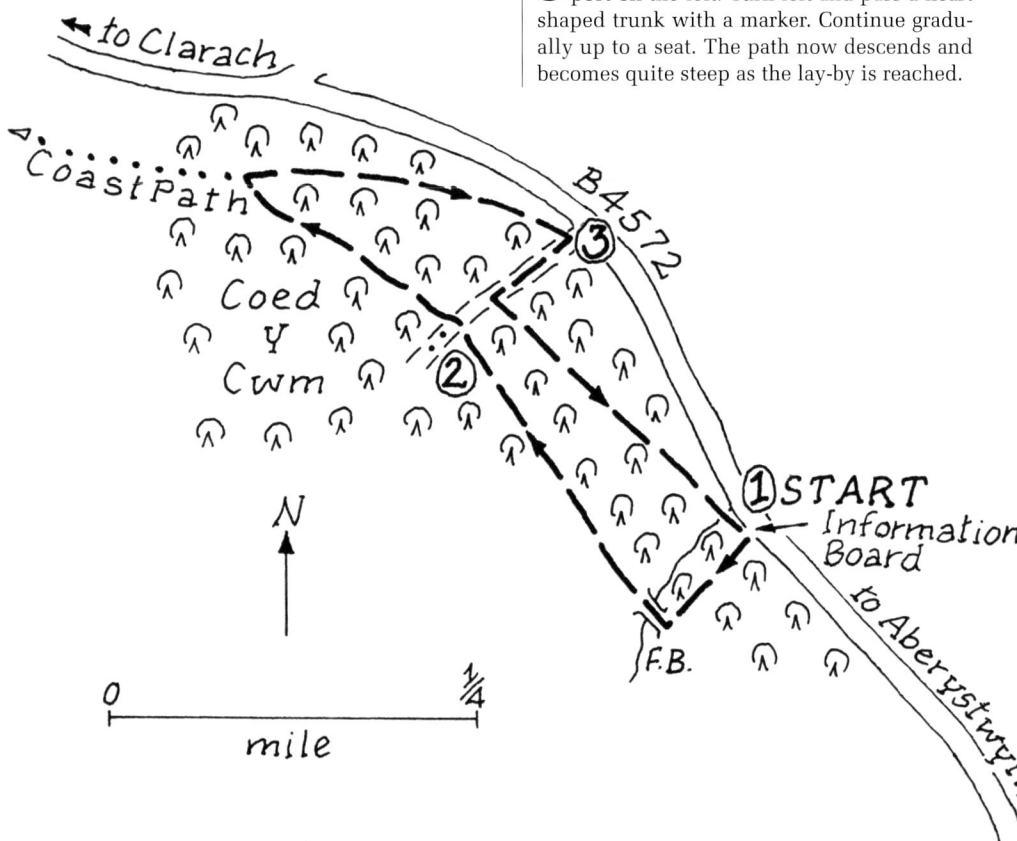

WALK 23
GOGERDDAN

DESCRIPTION A lovely, gentle 1¾ mile walk in predominantly broadleaf woodland with some very fine ancient trees. There are some great views as height is gained especially if you continue to the grassy summit of Allt Ddel. There is a very short section close to the Nant Clarach near the end of the walk. Allow 1½ hours.

START At the Forestry Commission car park close to Penrhyncoch.

DIRECTIONS From Aberystwyth follow the A44 east towards Llangurig for 2 miles. At the roundabout turn left on to the A4159. Continue along this road past the crossroads in Capel Dewi and turn right at the next crossroads towards Penrhyncoch. Turn left a mile further into the well-signed Forestry Commission car park.

The woodland gets its name from the nearby Plas Gogerddan, an old mansion owned by the Pryse family who were big silver and lead mine owners.

1 Follow the obvious signed path out of the car park and cross a footbridge that spans the Nant Clarach. At the marker post and path junction ahead continue on the right hand path to reach another path junction – marker post. Bear right and continue uphill to a seat by a marker post. Keep right on the main path to a marker post on the left. Walk ahead to another marker post on the left by a path junction. Continue straight ahead to a four-way junction. Cross straight over to reach a marker post on the right. Turn right here and walk up the quite steep hill, bearing to the right. Continue to a seat from where there is a good view. Turn left at a marker post. Continue along a lovely grassy path to yet another seat and marker post. There is a fine view of Bow Street below from here. Keep walking uphill and bear right at the next marker post and follow another lovely grassy path to the next marker post at a four-way junction. (If you are feeling energetic turn left here. Walk up the hill to a stile. Cross this and up the field at the top of which there are some marvellous panoramic views. Return to the four-way junction).

2 Continue straight ahead past the marker post seen to the right to the seat and four-way junction. Turn left and walk downhill to another four-way junction. Walk straight across with a marker post on your the and continue down to join the path of the outward walk. Turn right and continue to the marker post and path junction on the left. Turn left down the path and go along to the next marker post by a seat which again is on the main path of your outward walk. Bear right. At the next marker post, at a 'Y' junction, keep right (left is from the outward walk) to reach the Nant Clarach. It is possible to follow the left bank of this upstream for 50 yards. Pass below a very low canopy of beech and bear left away from the stream to join the path again. Turn right along it and right again at a marker post. Return to the car park over the footbridge.

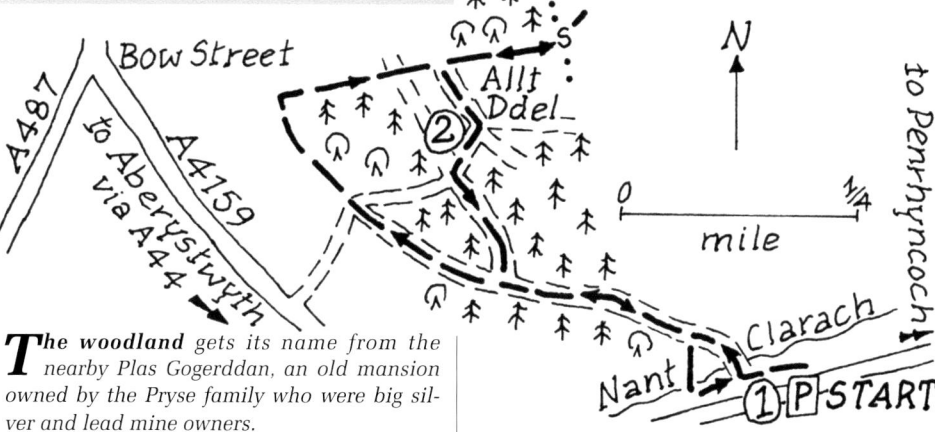

WALK 24
YNYS HIR

DESCRIPTION A pleasant 2½ miles figure of eight walk taking in the fine native woodland of the area. There is a plethora of bird life as well as some wonderful estuary views. The paths can be muddy during and after wet weather. There are hides from which you can observe the birdlife and even have lunch if the weather is somewhat unkind. The Domen Las Hide is closed from the end of February until the end of July to protect nesting Herons and Egrets. The walking time is around 1½ hours but the time spent here will be much longer, especially if watching the bird life. There is also a small charge, but there are toilets.

START From the car park for the RSPB Ynys Hir nature reserve.

DIRECTIONS From Machynlleth follow the A487 south towards Aberystwyth for 6 miles. Turn right at the sign indicating the reserve in Eglwysfach and follow the narrow road to the well signed car park. If coming from Aberystwyth along the A487 turn left immediately before crossing the bridge by the Furnace waterwheel. Turn left at the next road junction following signs to the car park as above.

1 From the car park walk towards the reception building. Walk in front of it and go through a gate. Turn left along the track and follow it up to reach a gate on the right where there is a marker post with a green arrow. Go through the gate and bear left following the often muddy path gradually uphill to the top of the rise. The path then descends through the fine sessile oak woodland to reach the Ynys Hir hide. *There is a great view of the Dyfi Estuary from here.* Continue along the path as it descends gradually to reach a gate.

2 Go through the gate to the track and turn right along it, indicated by a marker post and green arrow, to reach another similar post. Ignore the gate on the left where there is a marker post and red arrow. Keep following the track and walk through the gate 50 yards ahead. Continue up to a gate with a no entry sign. Bear right at a marker post and green arrow and walk through the gate 20 yards away. Follow the path, indicated by a marker post, as it bears left. Continue to go through a gate to join a track. Go right to a track junction. There is a marker post and green arrow here. The walk can be shortened here by turning right at the junction to return to the reception area and car park.

3 Turn left. Walk through the gate (there is a blue arrow on the reverse side of the marker post) and continue along the track. Go through a gate just before crossing the bridge spanning the Machynlleth to Aberystwyth railway line. Go through another gate at the far side. Turn left where there is a sign for the Saltings Hide. A good gravel path continues alongside the swamp on the left and passes through a gate. Continue on raised ground above the brackish water on the left. Cross a footbridge and through another gate just beyond. Continue to the hide. *There are great views here of the salt marshes, the estuary and the Tarren mountains.*

4 Continue along the grassy path that becomes very muddy for a very short distance. Go through a gate and across a footbridge, with a seat on the left. The path continues and is somewhat muddy in places to reach a finger post. Continue straight ahead towards Domen Las Hide. The path crosses through an area of sedge, where there is a marker post and blue arrow, and continues slightly up to go through a gate by a marker post. Continue to the hide situated close to the Afon Dyfi.

5 Return to the finger post and turn left up to the Marian Mawr Hide. Keep following the path to reach the railway bridge crossed previously. Return along the track to the track junction. Continue straight ahead to the gate on the left giving access to the reception area and car park.

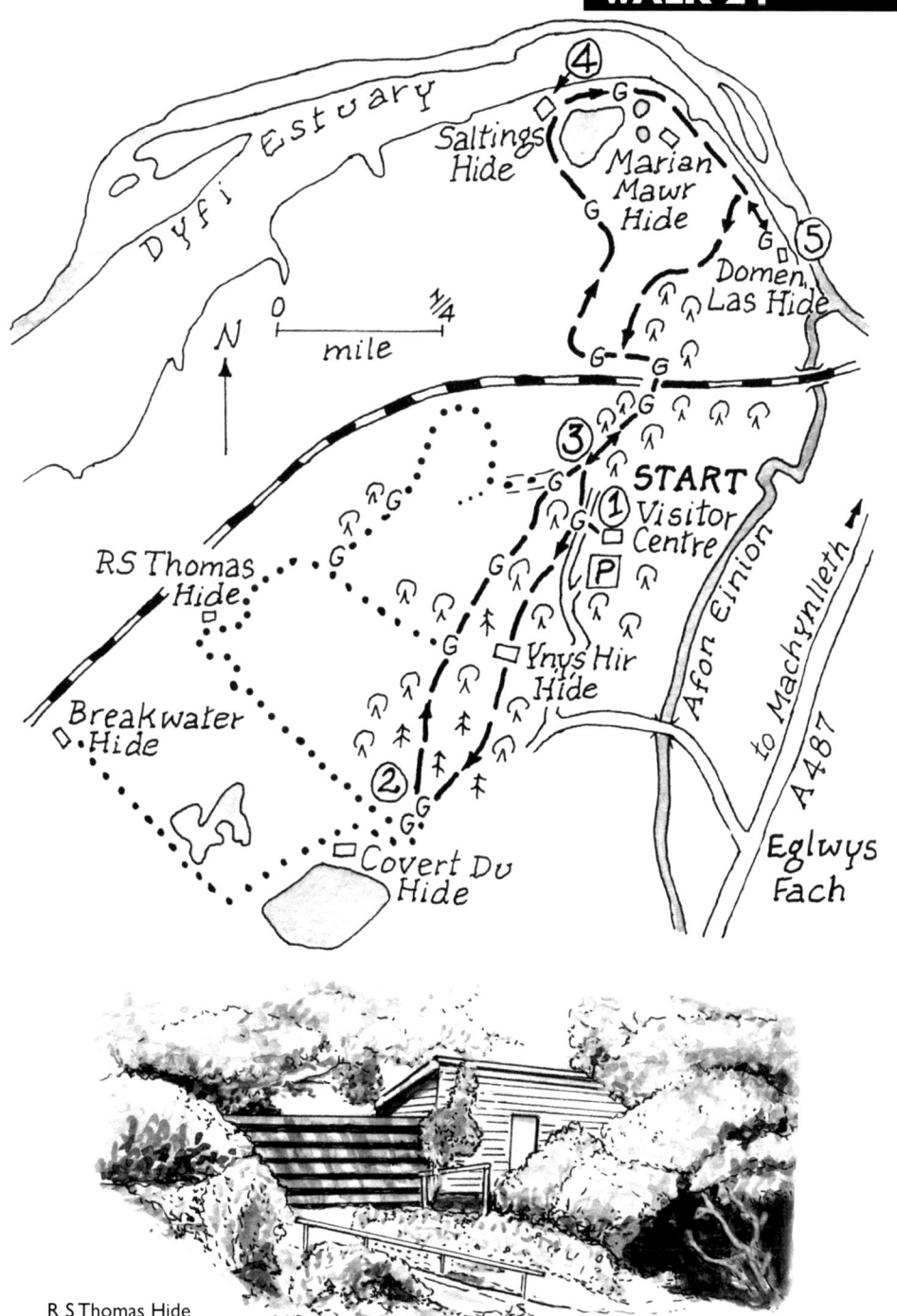

WALK 25
COED ALLT-GOCH & THE AFON LERI

DESCRIPTION One of the many attractions of this lovely 3¾ miles walk is that it is little known and is easy to follow. There are sea views, river views and some amazing woodland. Allow 2½ hours.
START From Dol-y-Bont.
DIRECTIONS From Aberystwyth follow the A487 towards Machynlleth. Turn left at Rhydpennau, signed to Borth, by the petrol station. Follow this road through Llandre into Dol-y-Bont. Turn right by the railway bridge. Drive down the steep hill, where, close to bottom some 150 yards from the turning there is parking for a couple of cars on the left. The approach from Machynlleth is to follow the A487 towards Aberystwyth and turning right just on entering Rhydpennau by the petrol station and following the directions above from there.

1 From your car walk along a level section of road for 150 yards to a footpath sign on the right. This is to the left of the private road. Turn right up the private road to a fence with 'Private' signs attached. Go over the stile on the right and follow the fenced path to another stile. Climb over this. The path turns through 90 degrees. Go over the next stile 20 yards ahead and up the steep grassy bank with steps. At the top of these bear left across the bottom edge of the steep field with a fence on the left, then gorse bushes. Continue, passing above the next caravan site to a stile. Climb over this. Keep going still above the caravan site to reach the edge of a wood and a fine rustic gate. Go through this and turn left. Descend to the caravan site. Turn left down the road and bear right at the 'Y' junction and left at the next junction to reach the footbridge spanning the Afon Leri on the right.

2 Cross the bridge. Turn right, and go through a kissing gate 50 yards further on. Continue up the path as it rises gradually to reach Fron-goch, a cluster of derelict farm buildings. Go through the gate and up to the large ruin. Just beyond this is a marker post. Bear right and go through another gate. Follow the grassy track from which there is a lovely view. The track becomes a grassy path across a large sloping field. Pass through the gate at the far side. Follow the track through mixed woodland to a turning circle, with a marker post ahead. DO NOT follow the track on the right but go up the path, to the left of the marker. Follow this path through some quite wonderful woodland. The path joins a track. Turn left along it. Where it starts to descend a waymarked path goes off to the left. Take this path. Just after it starts to descend go through a gate on the left waymarked to the Nant y Cwm.

3 Cross the stream and follow the path up. This becomes quite swampy but is easily avoided by veering to the right to join a track. Go left along the track with the Nant y Cwm on the left until a path leaves the wood by a ruin on the right. Cross the stream again below the ruin. Walk up the path and through a waymarked gate. Cross the field to another gate at the far side. Go through this onto the Alltgoch farm access track. Turn right through another gate and follow the track to the road.

4 Turn left on the road – there is a *great view of Aberdovey through the hedge on the right* – and when the road starts to descend a lovely view of the sea. Continue to a footpath sign on the left by the Henllys farm access track. Turn left and immediately left again through a gate. Bear right on the often muddy track. Following this above the farm buildings on the right. Go through a gate by the end of the buildings and close to a water trough. Bear right with a hedge to the left and go down to and over a waymarked stile. Follow the path below field level on

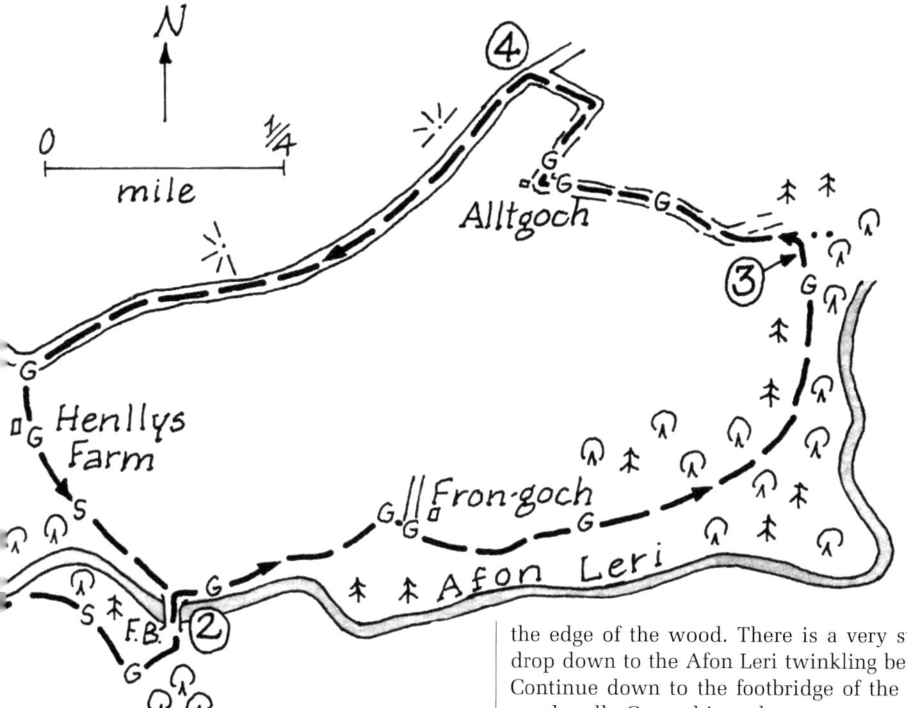

WALK 25

the edge of the wood. There is a very steep drop down to the Afon Leri twinkling below. Continue down to the footbridge of the outward walk. Cross this and retrace your steps back to Dol-y-Bont. *PLEASE NOTE: There is no way back to the village through the caravan site alongside the river.*

Coed Allt Goch

WALK 26
BLACK COVERT

DESCRIPTION This is a very pleasant 1¼ miles level walk that can be comfortably completed in 45 minutes and follows white marker posts. There are fine river views. The mixed woodland is rich in wildlife and there is a profusion of flowers, especially bluebells in spring. A covert is an area for raising game such as pheasants.

START At the Forestry Commission car park.

DIRECTIONS From Aberystwyth follow the A487 towards Cardigan. At Llanfarian. Turn left on to the A485 where there are signs for Llanilar and Trawsgoed. Continue along this road for 3 miles to reach Llanilar. At the roundabout in the village where the main road turns sharply right go straight ahead on to the B4575, signed for Trawsgoed. Continue along this road until you reach a junction where the road turns left over the bridge. Continue straight ahead. There is a parking sign indicating that the car park is 100 yards ahead. Turn left into it.

1 From the car park follow the gravel path past the information board and picnic tables. Continue in an upstream direction close to the Afon Ystwyth to a seat commanding a lovely view of the river. Keep following the path and cross a footbridge. Ignore the path on the right just before this. A rougher path continues to a marker post by a track on the right. Ignore this. Continue on the riverbank to pass another seat with another fine view of the river. The path now gradually moves away from the river. At the next marker post ignore the path on the right and continue across the footbridge. Keep going straight ahead, again ignoring a path on the right, to reach the riverbank once more. *Pause at the next seat for more river views.* The path now bears right 30 yards further on, where there is a marker post.

2 At the next marker post the obvious way is straight ahead. Instead turn right to the last footbridge you crossed. Go back across it and at the next marker post just beyond turn left. (This deviation avoids getting wet feet). Turn right at the next marker post and continue along a narrow track to another marker post at a 'Y' junction. Go up the left arm of the 'Y'. Just past a seat bear left by a marker post and follow the meandering path to reach a track junction at another marker post. Turn left along the track and follow it to bypass a gate on the right. Bear right at the next marker post which is close to the road and follow the path back to the car park.

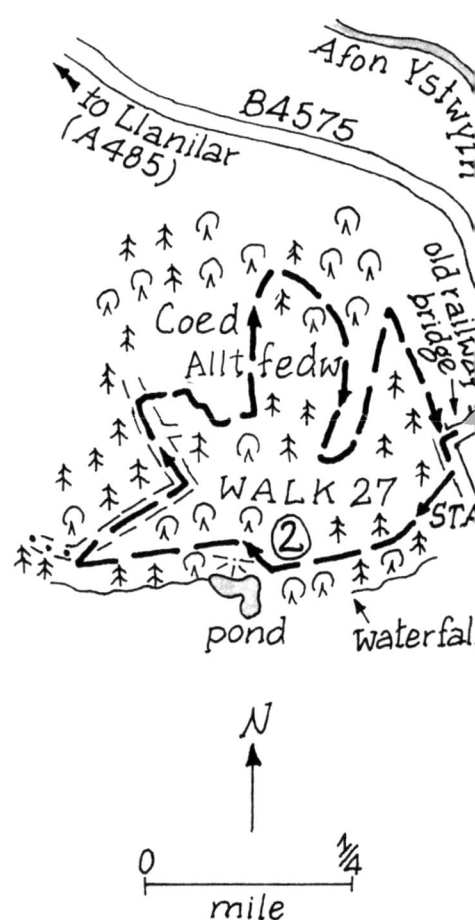

WALKS 26 & 27

WALK 27
COED ALLTFEDW

DESCRIPTION This is a good 2 miles walk which follows red marker posts. Although there are some steep sections the walk can be completed in 1¼ hours. The mixed woodland is rich in wildlife and there is a profusion of flsowers, especially bluebells in spring. There is a lovely small tumbling stream, a very pretty waterfall and a small lake.
START At the Forestry Commission car park.
DIRECTIONS As Walk 26.

1 From the car park follow the path downstream to reach the road. Turn right and walk over the bridge to reach the crossroads. Turn up to the left here following the narrow road up past a superb multi-limbed conifer on the right 40 yards up the road. Walk under the old railway bridge and continue straight ahead and pass the metal barrier. Walk up the forestry track to reach a marker post and an old post box! Turn left along the path where easier, less steep walking leads above a pretty and small tumbling stream on the left to arrive at a small waterfall. Steps lead up to a pretty but small lake at a path 'T' junction.

2 Turn right and follow the path past a seat on the left where there is a fine view across the lake. Keep following the path to arrive at a junction with a track and a marker post. Turn left and follow the track to a marker post on the right at a track junction. Turn right and go up bypassing a gate on the right. Walk up the track and around a hairpin bend. Continue to the next track junction just before a large metal box. Turn right at a marker post and walk up to a cleared area. Descend slightly and go around a sharp left hand bend to pass a marker post. The path continues down steps quite steeply to a track junction with a marker post. Turn right and continue down. Bear right at the next marker post and continue along to a path junction. Turn left here. Walk down steeply to where the path levels at a marker post. Continue ahead to join a track by a marker post. Turn right down the track and bypass the gate on the left to join the road of the outward walk. Turn left under the bridge back to the car park.

Red Admiral

Peacock

PRONUNCIATION

Welsh	English equivalent
c	always hard, as in **c**at
ch	as in the Scottish word lo**ch**
dd	as th in **th**en
f	as f in o**f**
ff	as ff in o**ff**
g	always hard as in **g**ot
ll	no real equivalent. It is like 'th' in then, but with an 'L' sound added to it, giving 'thlan' for the pronunciation of the Welsh 'Llan'.

In Welsh the accent usually falls on the last-but-one syllable of a word.

KEY TO THE MAPS

- ▬▶ Walk route and direction
- ▬▬ Metalled road
- ▬ ▬ ▬ Unsurfaced road
- • • • • Footpath/route adjoining walk route
- ～ River/stream
- ↟ ♁ Trees
- ▬■▬ Railway
- G Gate
- S Stile
- F.B. Footbridge
- ↘↖ Viewpoint
- P Parking
- T Telephone

THE COUNTRYSIDE CODE

- Be safe – plan ahead and follow any signs
- Leave gates and property as you find them
- Protect plants and animals, and take your litter home
- Keep dogs under close control
- Consider other people

Open Access
Some routes cross areas of land where walkers have the legal right of access under The CRoW Act 2000 introduced in May 2005. Access can be subject to restrictions and closure for land management or safety reasons for up to 28 days a year. Details from: www.naturalresourceswales.gov.uk.
Please respect any notices.

Published by **Kittiwake-Books Limited**
3 Glantwymyn Village Workshops, Glantwymyn, Machynlleth, Montgomeryshire SY20 8LY

© Text & map research: Des Marshall 2013, updated 2018.
© Maps & illustrations: Kittiwake-Books Ltd 2013
Drawings by Morag Perrott
Cover photos: Main: *Coed y Cwm*. Inset: *Coed y Brenin*. David Perrott

Care has been taken to be accurate. However neither the author nor the publisher can accept responsibility for any errors which may appear, or their consequences. If you are in any doubt about access, check before you proceed.

Printed by Mixam UK.

ISBN: **978 1 908748 13 3**